Voices of the
Undocumented

Val Rosenfeld and Flor Fortunati

Voices of the Undocumented
Copyright ©2015 Val Rosenfeld and Flor Fortunati

ISBN 978-1506-900-54-4 PRINT
ISBN 978-1506-900-55-1 EBOOK

LCCN 2015955105

October 2015

Published and Distributed by
First Edition Design Publishing, Inc.
P.O. Box 20217, Sarasota, FL 34276-3217
www.firsteditiondesignpublishing.com

Library of Congress Cataloging-in-Publication Data
Rosenfeld, Val, Fortunati Flor
   Voices of the undocumented / written by Val Rosenfeld and Flor
Fortunati.
   p. cm.
   ISBN 978-1506-900-54-4 pbk, 978-1506-900-55-1 digital

1. BIOGRAPHY & AUTOBIOGRAPHY / Cultural Heritage. 2. Personal
Memoirs. 3. POLITICAL SCIENCE / Public Policy / Social Policy. 4.
SOCIAL SCIENCE / Emigration & Immigration

V8897

CONTENTS

Introduction i

A Brief History of the Day Worker Center...iii

Chapter 1 Salvador's Story 2

Chapter 2 Ernesto's Story..20

Chapter 3 Lucía's Story...36

Chapter 4 Ruben's Story 52

Chapter 5 Aurora's Story...68

Chapter 6 José Luis's Story..78

Chapter 7 Laura's Story...98

Chapter 8 Carmen and Rocío's Stories...112

Chapter 8 (Continued) Rocío's Story..127

Epilogue..142

Discussion Questions 143

..... we are and always will be a nation of immigrants. We were strangers once, too.

Barack Obama

Introduction

For more than seven years, I have been teaching ESL ("English as a second language") as a volunteer at the Day Worker Center in Mt. View, California. When I first came to the Day Worker Center, I did not recognize its full purpose. I was retired and taking Spanish classes and was looking for an opportunity to practice the language. The Day Worker Center was a volunteer opportunity to get some real life Spanish experience and to contribute to the community at the same time. I soon discovered that very few of my friends knew about the Center or that such an organization even existed, let alone exactly what the Center did and whom it served.

A day worker center is a community-based organization that helps workers find day jobs. Although the center does not restrict who can register for their services, in the San Francisco Bay Area it primarily serves a Latino immigrant population. There are approximately 70 such day worker centers throughout the United States. While these centers vary in their locations and administration, each center aims to provide jobs for service workers - to help such workers, who would otherwise stand on street corners, come in off the streets into a supportive environment. Employers in the area are then encouraged to hire their day workers from the centers, rather than off the street.

Over these seven years, I have been responsible for two ESL classes a week at the Day Worker Center of Mountain View – a beginning class and an advanced class. During this time, I have heard small parts of many of the workers' life stories. As I got to know the workers better, I found that I wanted to hear their whole stories – where they came from, how they got here, and how they found their place in this country and community. Since many of the workers have limited proficiency with English, I realized that they needed to tell their stories in their native language in order to convey all the details and the associated emotions. When Flor Fortunati, who is from Argentina and thus fluent in Spanish, joined me as a volunteer teacher at the Day Worker Center, she felt the same draw to the workers' stories that I had experienced. Together, we had the ability to interview the workers and to hear their stories in their own language and in their own words.

We selected men and women from a variety of Latin American countries to interview. At first, many of the workers were reluctant to talk about their pasts. Perhaps, the workers worried that by telling their stories, they would endanger their status in the Unites States, as many of them are undocumented. Perhaps the workers worried that middle-class Americans would not understand their hardships and experiences. But, once Flor and I started interviewing them, they quickly opened up. They wanted someone to be interested, someone to understand what they had experienced in their efforts to create new lives for themselves and their families. As the workers became increasingly comfortable speaking of their pasts, we discovered how moving their stories were and how justifiably proud the workers were of their accomplishments. And, at the same time, we found that knowing the details of their lives made us feel closer to them as students and as people and neighbors.

We recorded all of the interviews in Spanish, transcribed them and then translated them into English. We have made every effort to allow each worker to tell his or her story in his or her own words. To preserve the integrity of their stories, we have presented them as a narrative, as the workers have told them to us. Only first names have been used and some names and locations have been changed, and pictures omitted, at the request of the worker. We believe this documentation of oral history is important. You must know the stories to truly know the people.

A Brief History of the
Day Worker Center

In the San Francisco Bay Area, the cities of Palo Alto, Mountain View and Los Altos, along with local police departments, openly support the Day Worker Center. This has not always been the case, however.

In 1994, California voters overwhelmingly approved Proposition 187, also known as Save Our State. Proposition 187 was a ballot initiative to establish a state-run citizenship screening system and prohibit undocumented immigrants from access to health care, public education and a range of other social services. The proposition passed by a wide margin and its passage immediately resulted in wide-spread opposition. Legal challenges to the new law soon followed. Three days after the passage of Proposition 187, a federal judge entered a temporary restraining order blocking the enforcement of the law. Within a month, a permanent injunction was issued finding the proposition unconstitutional and blocking all provisions of the law. Specifically, the judge found that the law infringed on the federal government's exclusive jurisdiction over immigration-related matters.

The injunction against Proposition 187 did not change the community's attitude toward day laborers, unfortunately. Around the same time, residents in the California cities of Mountain View and Los Altos, along with their police departments, complained about immigrants congregating on the street corners in search of job opportunities. In an effort to address these divisive issues, a community lawyer in the area brought together people from various constituencies, including, elected officials, religious leaders and residents, to create a focus group to develop the concept of a physical day worker center. The initial Center operated within the rectory of a small church, but, after its initial success, moved to another building in a more central business location in Mountain View. It operated there until 1999, when the cities of Los Altos and Mt. View each passed an ordinance banning employers from picking up day workers from street corners, thereby making it illegal for residents and businesses to hire a large segment of the undocumented worker population seeking employment.

While the Center aimed to get workers off street corners, its fate remained uncertain as well. When the Center's lease expired in 2001, the landlord elected not to renew it. With the loss of the lease, the Day Worker Center literally disappeared. Virtually overnight, there was no Center, no computers, no telephone, no work opportunities, nothing. During the next few months, the organizers of the Day Worker Center collected signatures, held marches, and went to the city councils. Finally, the Center's organizers found assistance with a large law firm in Palo Alto, California. Lawyers from Morrison and Foerster and MALD (Mexican American Legal Defense), working together, were able to successfully challenge the city ordinances. The cities were forced to pay the Center's legal fees and to compensate the organization for all the damage it had sustained. This success served as an important victory for the Center and for undocumented workers' rights.

In 2002, after this successful legal victory, the Day Worker Center re-opened. Throughout the next nine years, the Center operated from various rooms in local churches. By 2011, the Center had raised enough funds through private donations to purchase a former laundromat in Mountain View, where it established its new headquarters as a non-profit, 501(c)(3) Corporation. The Center refurbished the building to include an office, a greeting area, a great room (with tables and chairs, a library area and computer area), a kitchen, and a classroom. The Center currently employs a paid director and two assistants and has an annual budget of approximately $150,000, which is funded through a combination of grants and private donations.

Today, 60-80 day workers use the Center's service. Approximately 10% of the workers are non-Latinos, primarily from Ethiopia and other parts of Africa. Another, smaller portion of workers were born and raised in the United States, but have turned to the Center in search of day employment. Regardless of the worker's origins, the Center has become part of their lives.

Despite the success of the Center, numerous immigrants still look for work on street corners. Some of these workers wish to negotiate for jobs by themselves, preferring to avoid the rules of the Center, such as wearing a "uniform" (workers are required to wear a Day Worker T-Shirt to all jobs) and participating in the obligatory English classes. These workers prefer to handle it themselves. They want to be outside and feel strong enough to communicate with employers on their own.

Finding jobs for the day workers remains the primary goal of the Center. Each morning, workers put their names on a list (the first ones to arrive are first on the list) that is used to assign jobs. When employers call or come by the Center, the workers who arrived earliest get priority. Employers typically seek workers for manual labor: moving, cleaning, gardening and some minor construction. These are some of the hardest, most grueling jobs and are poorly paid. Hourly wages are $12 - $15 (depending on the skills necessary for the job) for a minimum of 4 hours.

In addition to its job-finding function, the Center has become a community center for immigrants. Workers come to the Center and ask basic questions, such as: "Can you please translate this document?" "Can you help me find a school for my children?" "Where can I find medical care for my family?" "How can I find an apartment to rent or a room to share?" The Center strives to create an environment in which the workers feel safe asking for help and sharing their problems and concerns. The Center offers workshops on consumer rights, tenant rights and civil rights. Families are also welcome, including children. The workers can come and eat here, share a meal, and talk to other people while they wait for work.

Many workers leave their spouses and children in their home countries, not wanting to raise their children in the U.S. Most of the workers just want to make enough money to support their families and, eventually, return to their countries of birth. They miss their homes, their families, and their own culture. Unfortunately, these workers often arrive with unrealistic expectations of their opportunities in the U.S., believing they can stay a few years, and pay back all of the money they owe (often thousands of dollars paid to the coyotes for bringing them across the border) and save some additional money for their family. They think that a year's work will allow them to return to their families in their native countries with enough money to start a business. Expectations are that workers will be able to send back a few hundred dollars a month – which is a great deal more than they can earn at home. They are willing to live five or six men to an apartment, skip meals, and wear second hand clothes in an effort to save money to send home.

But the years go by. One year turns into two and then three. The passage of time often erodes family relationships, which simply cannot stand the huge time, distance and financial burdens placed on them. Workers' expectations prove unrealistic. The husband comes with dreams and hopes. The wife stays back home, waiting for money. The workers try and stay connected to their families, but often a feeling of impotence and shame arises when they cannot provide adequately for them. Then, their families just disappear. It is a very common story, and happy endings are rare.

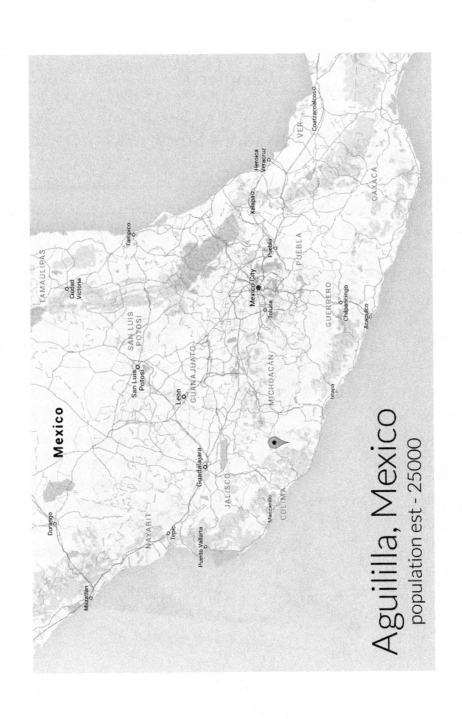

Aguililla, Mexico
population est - 25000

Chapter 1

Salvador's Story

"In Mexico, where I lived, there was a great deal of violence. This was the main reason I decided to try to go to the U.S. The authority is for sale in Mexico. I've seen people murder my friends in front of me. I've seen them fall. Once a friend of mine was killed beside me. These guys arrived, and when I looked and saw who was coming, my friend was right beside me. He had told me what was going on, and as soon as I moved, they shot him. I moved so that they wouldn't shoot me and the bullet flew right beside my head. It was a problem concerning 'skirts'. My friend had told me everything that was going on and said 'my friend will come to kill me' and after a while, we saw him coming and my friend said, 'there he comes, there he comes,' and a minute later, he was dead.

"On another occasion I saw soldiers kill four men. The soldiers have authorization to shoot anyone that opposes them. Because if the soldiers come and try to disarm you and you show them your gun, you'll get shot and killed. That time, four friends went down the street with loud music and bearing guns; they were criminals. The soldiers waited for them on the corner and as they arrived the soldiers told them to raise their hands. One of the friends, his name was Rogelio, without more ado, took his gun and shot the commander. He shot and hit him. When he showed his gun, he was told, 'raise your hands,' he shot the officer, he shot the lieutenant, and hit him in the chin and shoulder. But the soldiers were aiming their guns at the men. Then, when the gun thundered, the soldiers shot. All four friends fell.

"There were also a lot of drugs when I was growing up. Yes there was, yes. But there was not the slaughter of people like there has been since ten years ago. There were drugs in the hills and the soldiers went and brought a lot of drugs and a lot of people tied up, from the mountain, from the hills. But there weren't as many murders as there have been in the last ten years. We didn't have that. Drugs, yes, lots and lots. I'm more afraid to go back home right now. It scares me because now they pick people up and one walks to the truck and the next day or in two days' time you are already dead in a ditch or on the mountain. They kill and ditch them, so that scares me now."

Salvador is 64 years old. Although he describes himself as the smallest in his large family, he is 5 feet 11 inches tall, 185 pounds and solidly built, with a strong jaw, salt-and-pepper hair and a full moustache. He was born in 1950 in Aguililla, in the state of Michoacán, in western Mexico. To the east is Mexico City; to the west, the Pacific Ocean. The name 'Michoacán' is from Nahuatl, a Uto-Aztecan language spoken in central Mexico since the 7th century AD, and it means 'place of the possessor of fish,' referring to those who fish on Lake Patzcuaro.

Today Michoacán is a region of drug production, sex-trafficking, oil theft, kidnapping, gun running and extortion. But in 1950, when Salvador was born, Augililla was a sleepy little village in central Michoacán. "Although I was born in Aguililla, my family moved to a ranch after I was born and stayed on the ranch, called Reparito, for three years. My dad worked planting corn. Then we went back to the town, to Aguililla, and then from Aguililla we went to another ranch, La Laja. We lived in La Laja possibly fifteen years. We went back and forth from the ranch to town, depending on the situation. In May, we would go to the ranch to plant and in December, after the harvest, we went back to the town. We did this for many years and then in 1969 we returned to the village of Aguililla and stayed.

"My father had rented the land on the ranch but owned a house in town. The house had a dirt floor. It had no bathroom and did not have any electric light. I remember we used candles or oil lighting. My grandfather, my mom's dad, and my mom's mom lived in the same town. The town of Aguilla was very limited - eight or ten houses at most. But when one is young you can have fun with everything. Even if you don't have anything to eat tomorrow, a child is happy, having fun. As an adult, it changes and when you are old, it changes more.

"All the families were very large. My mother stayed at home. We were nine children, five boys and four girls and I was the fifth child. My uncle, the brother of my mother, had eleven children! Another uncle had 14, and yet another brother of my mother, 10, and another brother, 6. They all lived nearby in the village. In Aguililla, I met a lady with 26 children; 26 from the same man and they all became adults. They are not all alive now, some have been killed, and some are miscreants. But their parents saw them all till adulthood. It is amazing.

"The first part of life is the most beautiful. We had little money, I wore patched clothes. I wore shoes for the first time at age 20. I used to wear *guarachitas*. I owned only one pair of shoes, that's all, and few clothes, two or three changes only. And my mom patched my clothes over and over.

"I only went to school for a little time. I had an aunt who taught me and my dad paid her. Three of my brothers and two of my sisters went there to learn. My dad was paying her per month, but only for a short time - five months and no more. I grew up speaking Spanish. I can read Spanish a little, not very fast, but I read. My younger siblings went to the government school. It was easier then, when we lived in town, because when we lived on the farm, there was no school. There were only four houses on the ranch, and there was another ranch far away. It took an hour of walking to go to school. Two younger brothers went to school, but the biggest, no, they didn't.

"I began working, when I was 10 years old, - less than 10 years. My dad earned money by sowing seed, and also herding mules and cattle. We went with my dad to plant corn, and then also helped with the horses, too. I learned how to ride horses and mules. I also worked during harvesting, herding mules loaded with corn and gathering the *breña* to burn, too. There was always work to do. When we were in town my dad would bring firewood on mules to sell, and we helped. And when we were back in town, some of us would be hired for the day. Sometimes when I went to work there were unpleasant odors and thorns, but it was only a day. It passes, it passes. A hot day, but it passes, it passes. It's all good. All my sisters stayed home and helped in the kitchen. Two of my sisters made clothes, with sewing machines, and people paid them to make clothes.

"In the village, after we worked, we played at night, in the center of the square. My many cousins and I ran around over there under the trees, and we threw stones at the animals. I liked to go play with nuts as balls. There's a tree that bears nuts in the center of the square and we gathered some nuts to play. Nuts, if you gather some and store them where there's no sun and don't get them wet, they last 10 years and you can eat them. They last a long time and nothing happens, nothing happens. A grain of corn or rice too, if you keep it dry, walk away, 50 years later, you plant it and it grows corn. They last long, last long, 50 years. We played with walnuts, and since there were plenty, we filled large bags, and we kept them there.

"One year, in December – December 12th, it was a holiday and there was a party in Aguililla, and I was penniless. My dad had cornfields and harvested and sold and collected all the money to sustain a large family. My dad would not spend the money on himself; no, we were nine, plus my dad and my mom. We all ate, all eleven, we all spent; the crops were for our house. Two days before the 12th, a friend of mine asked me, 'Will you help me harvest? We'll finish in a day.' 'Uh, really?' I said. I did not have any money and I had a girlfriend who was my first girlfriend. Well, I'll work because I don't want to be penniless on the 12th. We went to work and started early in the morning and ended when it was getting dark. The next day was December 12th. I got home and I went to bathe at night in a river, a river in December is cold, but anyway, I bathed there in the cold river. My friend lived in a small house near me. He told me, 'After a while I'll bring you the money.' 'Okay.' I bathed, returned, and he did not show up. The next day, on the 12th, I met him there and he said, 'You know what? The man that was going to pay me gave me nothing. He did not pay me.' I had no money to go for a walk with my girlfriend, or to invite her for a soda. But, I didn't get angry, I did not blame him. I got paid, but two or three days afterwards. But that beautiful day, there was nothing. These are little things that one remembers.

"I never served in the army. No, no, no. It was an option, but my dad was a bit closed. Two of my older brothers went marching. But I did not. One day I told my dad, 'I'm going to subscribe for military service' and he said: 'No! That does not work, that's no good.' And that was it. It was not mandatory, well I never heard anyone say: 'They took them to the military.' No, I've never heard it. Maybe in other times, maybe, but I do not remember them taking anyone. My dad was closed-minded. He also did not know how to read; he could read in Spanish a little bit because he taught himself a little when he was older.

"My dad would not let us go to work for a government company. He said, 'No.' In Mexico, there are large companies, where there are military soldiers protecting the company and the company pays them compensation. My dad was opposed to 'those companies from the government.' My dad was like that. But after I asked him five hundred times, I told him, 'I'm going to work' and he decided. 'Ok, go.' My dad always had those ideas about companies with the government. He thought that it does not work. But my dad was wrong.

"So eventually we all worked for large companies - my four brothers and my dad. With all of us working, our economic situation changed. My brothers went to work in construction, building houses. Then I went to work at a road construction company. After that, I went to work at a sawmill and worked there for three years, cutting wood to make tables.

"Life changed; it became a little bit better. As it improved we were able to add a bathroom to the house, as well as lighting, and wooden floors and a stove. Everything was a bit better.

"However, after three years, the sawmill closed. It was a big company, with a very large sawmill, with a huge production. When it closed all the workers got money, this much for you, this much for you. For a short while I worked fixing truck tires. I would fix the tires that were punctured. The company was a sawmill, but it also had truck maintenance and I was in charge of that. I was the *llantero*. They hired me for that, because I had worked for three years, and at the mill they heard I was out of work and they looked for me and hired me.

"And that was the last job there in Mexico, and that was it and then I came here. That is how I got the money to come to the United States. I had wanted to come to the U.S. for many years, but I did not have enough money. So what stopped me was the economic situation. I did not dare to borrow money to come here. After I worked at the sawmill, when it was over, they gave money to everyone and I said to myself, 'this money, is for this,' and with that money I came to the U.S. But I wanted to come, 8, 10 years before I finally came. I told my dad, 'Well, I'm leaving tomorrow,' and he asked where I was going? I said, 'To the U.S.' He said, 'But what are you going to do there, just go and open your mouth there?' 'No, well, I am leaving.' 'Okay, Okay,' he said. My mother was sad, but my dad wasn't. He was sad, he just didn't show it. My mother cried, but my father didn't.

"I came to the U.S. illegally in May, 1979. I took a bus to Tijuana from Aguililla. It took two days. I only had the clothes I had on, and one change of clothes in a bag. In Tijuana, I paid a coyote on the border $250 to help me jump the fence and cross over into California. Back then there wasn't a big fence like right now. Back then there was a regular fence, a wire fence; it was low, and you jumped over it. It was barbed wire, but it was low. Right now the fence is 12 feet high, and made of steel – so it's difficult now. After we climbed the fence, we walked a little, one hour, maybe two. Then we got to a house on the U.S. side of the border - a house the coyote controlled. We remained hidden in the house for four days. After that, a car was sent to pick us up; we got in the trunk of the car and went to Los Angeles in the trunk, lying there. The money I paid the coyote brought me across and included everything. After I crossed, they brought me up to Redwood City (California), on the Greyhound bus. I came across the border four times, as I will explain later. Each time was slightly different. Once I paid the coyote only to Los Angeles, and went from Los Angeles to the Bay Area on the Greyhound. Other times I paid to Redwood City, and it was included in the coyote's, price.

"It was not difficult to cross. Just a little bit of walking. We just walk and hide, and walk again for 30 minutes and hide, but it was not long. Some people come by Arizona, and they walk for 10 hours. We were a group of 25, 30 people and children. The guide there was ahead. One by one we followed. It was dark, at night. In the evening, at 8:00, as it got dark, we crossed, and after a while we hid. We could see a plane above us, but it did not see us. There we would wait till dawn. We were picked up in a car, two or three cars because there were many of us, and from there we drove to Los Angeles. That was the first time.

"The United States was just as I thought it would be. They told me that it was clean, beautiful, lighted streets, and cement sidewalks, impressive stores, very different from Mexico. It ended up being as I thought it was. It was what I expected. "The most difficult time was the first year I came. I came to Redwood City, penniless and knowing nothing. I brought one pair of shoes. One or two weeks later, a cousin asked me to go to K-Mart to shop. They are in Redwood City and here in Santa Clara there were some. My cousin asked me to come; he was with his wife, and we were neighbors here. He said, 'Come to K-Mart.' We went together, and when we got in the store my cousin started shopping with his wife there. I only had one U.S. dollar. There were some shirts hanging there at 99 cents, but when I go to pay, because of the tax, it was more than one dollar. Ninety-nine cents, but with the tax, it cost slightly more than one dollar I had. Well, I could not buy it. I left the store and my cousin stayed there.

"I got out and I walked. I knew where to wait for the bus. I knew where I was walking and I arrived at Middlefield Road. There in Redwood City, there was a gentleman, sitting there, a Chilean, sitting there, 'Hey! Is the truck (bus) about to arrive?' He said, 'It is,' and I sat and waited, but since I left the store I was thinking and thinking about the situation that I was in, and thinking and thinking. And as I sat there I was crying, I was crying, thinking I did not have money. And the Chilean said, 'What's wrong? Are you crying?' 'No, no, I'm not crying. I have dust in my eyes.' 'Hey you're crying!' he said again. 'Yes, I'm crying, yes, I'm crying' 'What's wrong?' 'Look, I have no job, nor do I have money. I went to buy a shirt and I did not have enough money.' He said, 'Are you sick?' 'No, no, I'm not sick.' He said, 'Do not worry, you've got your health, you're young, do not worry.' Well yes, I thought. I'm not sick, I can work. And that helped me a lot. He helped me a lot.

"After that, I was working two or three days a week as a day worker. Then I had no more work and then in a few more days there was more work. It was very limited. I saved and saved. Rent was $60 per month. When you don't have a job, it's a lot, a lot right? I earned $90 in total. They paid $2.90 per hour and at that time I did not pay taxes. I didn't pay anything else. $90. It was limited, limited living. I was never hungry, but there were times when you didn't get to eat until late at night.

"I was here 6 months and then I was caught. When one is arrested, it's a horrible thing. Immigration caught me in the park. I lived in Redwood City and came to see volleyball games in a park in Mt. View. I like that a lot, watching volleyball; every day I went to watch, almost every day. I had just arrived there at Rengstorff Park and Immigration was there gathering people. They were heading out and we ran into each other. So I came here to the park and as I was arriving here, they were catching people and they caught me. There was a big truck and two or three small trucks. The truck stopped and the driver of the truck got off the truck and the others who were with him arrived fast and they got out their guns. The driver cried, 'Amigo! Amigo!' and I stopped. I had a friend who had a similar van. That particular day I went there because he needed help fixing a detail on it, and when I looked I thought it was my friend with his van. But it was Immigration. They asked for my papers – I had none. I got on the truck; there were 22 people.

"They arrested me on Sunday and I was taken to Santa Rita. They moved me on Monday afternoon. We got to the line in downtown Mexicali; we stayed a while longer and then were sent by bus to Guadalajara. There they let me go and from there it took six more hours to get to my village, Aguililla. I went by bus, I had some money and I bought the ticket there, for $24.

"The Border Patrol did not take anything away from me, they just searched me. They treated me very well. I had very few things, only the clothes I was wearing, because all of my things were in my apartment. I had only a few things there - six months' worth of things. I called a cousin of mine and asked if she were coming back to Mexico, please bring me the things that I have there in the apartment. She brought me my clothes. I would have lost it all, but then it was only two or three shirts and clothing. I was lucky, though. I had a check for $150 in my pocket when they caught me. $150 in a check and $150 in cash. $300 with the check and the cash. I had them with me because I got paid on Saturday and I pocketed the check and was walking around and they caught me and I had the check on me and $150 in cash. Thankfully I didn't have to return to Mexico without any money.

"I crossed back to the U.S illegally again. The second time, it was the shortest stretch. We walked for two hours. A car picked us up and took us to Redwood City. And the third time was also short. We went by car. The third time, after crossing, we went into a house and spent 2 days there. In the house, there was food and water. We were four or five people. And the fourth time, because I got to jump 4 times, in 1979, 1980, 1983 and 1985, four times. The last time we walked during the day, we were lucky. We ran like 30 minutes, and bam! We got to the car, fast; it was two in the afternoon, it was the easiest. There are always many animals, but I am not afraid of animals, I was not scared.

"Well, I had a cousin in the Bay Area and I spoke to him and he asked, 'How are you coming?' 'In a Greyhound.' 'When you arrive, I'll be there waiting, here in Redwood City,' and he was waiting for me. Well I got luckier when I came back the final time in 1985. It changed because I got here and a bit later I got a job. I started to work after three days and that work was for two years. Then I left, by then the situation had changed.

"I met Esther, originally from DF Mexico City, in 1985. I was 35 and she was two years older, 37. She worked in Cupertino, and I worked and lived in Redwood City. We met on the #22 bus. It was Sunday and I came from Redwood City and was going to San Jose. She got on the bus at San Antonio and El Camino. When we met, we started talking, and continued the conversation until today. No, we're a couple, but not married; we've been together for about 25 years. She was 38 when my baby, Alicia, was born in the United States.

"By amnesty, in 1987, I became a resident. Esther got her residency later. When I met her she was illegal–she had over-stayed her visa. I was a resident when I met her and she was illegal, but when I met her she was applying for residency and then managed to get it, but many years after I met her.

"Then, in 1990, I could not work for a few years. I had been working for a roofing company for about a year when I had an accident and I burned my hand and arm with that black tar that you throw on houses–that is why I have all the scars on my right arm. The pain wasn't too bad, but in my mind I was traumatized by what I saw. As soon as the firemen arrived I got an injection and the pain was over. But in my mind it was horrible. I had to have surgery - a skin graft. I was 40. The ambulance took me to the hospital and I stayed for fifteen days in the hospital. The company gave me $800 per month for eight months while I was out of work–State Compensation. Two checks of $400. It was very little. When I was out of the hospital, I contacted a lawyer about the accident. He took the case but it did not help. I only got $6000 after 5 years. I was sent back to work after eight months. But I was not well, so I did not go to work. The doctor gave me a letter and said, 'Take it to the company where you work,' but I didn't take it because I did not feel competent. So the allowance was cut. I did not go back to that job. I never went back.

"When Alicia was five months old, Esther went to Mexico because her father became ill. She went to Mexico because she had originally come to the U.S. with a visa, and she came and went with a visa. Except the visa was now expired. She stayed in Mexico for 5 months and told me, 'I'll arrive at SFO [airport], wait for me at the airport. I'm taking a few things for you to help me with.' I arrived at SFO, 30 minutes earlier than her arrival. The plane arrived, people kept coming and she didn't come through the gates. I said to a woman: 'Is a lady with a one-year-old girl coming?' She said, 'She has been stopped there and they are asking her many questions.' It was immigration services, at the airport. Then the immigration worker from the airport came and said, 'Salvador! Come here to say hello to her, because we are sending her back.' And he asked me for my green card. I showed it. My wife was already there, and crying. They made her go back to Mexico with the baby, but it didn't affect her green card application. It was lucky they didn't reject her application. Then he said, 'You can talk to her for 15 minutes, because we are sending her back right now on the same plane she came.' And we were talking and the officer said, 'Time for you to go,' and gave me the things she brought for me. She spent three months there and came back by paying a coyote. Before she returned, I met Esther in Tijuana. Alicia was born here, in the U.S., so she had no trouble passing. She gave me the girl there, in Tijuana, and later she paid a coyote to cross. Afterwards, Esther got her green card, because she hadn't lost her status.

"We live together in Santa Clara. First in an apartment for a while and right now we have lived for eleven years in a three room house that we own. Esther cleans houses and does housekeeping. She works Monday to Saturday usually and Sunday occasionally. Now I work as a day worker. We divide the expenses between my daughter, my wife and me, and more or less we manage. Our main expenses are the house payment. The food is not so expensive. Food is really more expensive in Mexico than here, more expensive in comparison to what one makes. Because here, an ordinary day for a worker is $100; not too bad. With $100 I'll eat 10 times, I'll go to eat at a restaurant, but not a fancy restaurant. In Mexico, one day's pay equals two times eating in a restaurant. Look, what a comparison, twice to ten, it's a big difference, big difference, so the food is not such a big expense—it is the rent.

"We were able to buy a house because my wife had money for a down payment. In Mexico, my wife had a license to rent space in a building that held a market. When she came to the U.S. she sold the license for that building space. From there she got the money for the house's down payment, $100,000. We make monthly payments to the bank of $2,000. We do not pay much, because we gave $100,000 as a down payment. My wife wanted to put $200,000 down. We have paid for the first 11 years out of 25.

"Esther wants to be herself. I will put up with everything that I can, because I have patience. Look, when you have an issue with your husband, it should be discussed just between the two of you. When my daughter was three years old, Esther kicked me out. She kicked me out for three days. Those were bad days, the days I felt most alone in life. One day we were talking, we sat down to dinner at the table, and I cannot remember what we were arguing about, not that I wouldn't want to tell you, but I do not remember. We had an argument. I do not feel it was a strong argument, but she slaps me across my face. It was not an argument, it wasn't strong, but the emotions were strong, so I slapped her back. More or less the same way she hit me. She said nothing - I just saw her face, angry, she got up and went into the room. Then I had dinner and I got up and she was crying there. 'Go away,' she said 'Get out of here.' I pretended not to hear.

"The next day I was not working because I was incapacitated by the roofing accident. My girl was about three years old then. The next day, Esther got up early, she worked every day, seven days a week then, and she went to work. I was there in the house. At six, seven o'clock, in the evening she arrived, and said, 'Hey, didn't you hear what I told you last night? You need to get out of here.' The next day she went, as usual, to work. That day I went to walk my baby down the street and I was crying and walking, and my child asked, because my little girl learned Spanish and English very well from the beginning, she said, 'Hey Dad, are you crying?' 'No, my daughter, I am not crying, there's dust in my eyes.' I walked and my girl asked me again, 'Are you crying, Dad?' 'No, it's just dust.' But she noticed. That was at noon, my wife was working, and I arrived with my daughter, from a little walk of half an hour. I started to wrap my stuff there, make a packet of clothes, a small package. My sister lived in Redwood City, and I called her and asked if my brother-in-law was there. Her husband was my friend. ' Ask my friend, when he arrives, if he can call me?' A few hours later, I called again, and when I called he was there. 'My friend, what happened?' he asked. *Compadre*, I want to ask you for a favor, without prejudice. Can you give me permission to stay there in your house alone, because my wife gave the apartment back and she's going to Mexico with my girl?' I said that, but it was a lie. So I said, 'And if you do me the favor to receive me, please come get me right now, I have everything packed,' because I had only a few things.

"I didn't even have $5.00. I didn't have a job, and the help I had, the monthly payment from the accident, had been cut. I got there at night and cried all night long. I was there three days. And then Esther calls the house. She also knew how to cut hair, she learned in Mexico. She said to my brother-in-law 'Hey *compadre*, it's been a long time since I gave your children haircuts, how are they?' 'Oh! They look awful,' he answered. 'No one has cut their hair other than you when you came.' She said, 'I am coming over to cut their hair.' But she just wanted to go where I was. She arrived there and we started talking, and after five hours, she had cut the kids' hair. 'We're leaving, *compadre*,' she said. 'Come here,' she said to me, in the other room, because there were people there. 'Come over here,' and we went into the other room, 'What do you want?' I said 'Hey, I want you to forget what happened, I want you to forget it, and I want you to come back.' I was not deaf, either. Those three days were heavy. These are things one remembers, as you know.

"Anyway, I never drank, not young nor old. Yes, I like drinking, but I do not like it when I see what one does when he's drunk. I've been drunk twice in my life, once in Mexico and over here the year I came here. I got

13

drunk there once and four years later I got drunk for the second time here. Since then, I've said, 'No more.' It's been 34 or 35 years of that. Never again. Why? Because a person who is drunk will spit out words like an old guitar. A person, when he's drunk, demands things that make no sense at all. If I'm drunk I'll say: 'Hey! That day I found you, you did not greet me.' What kind of claims are those? 'Hey! The other day I asked for a cigar, you had one and refused me.' This is not an appropriate demand, these things are simple things, but claims have been made. So they are claiming things without sense, without a case, this has led me to not drink.

"Our daughter, Alicia, is now 24 years old and lives with us. She went to school in the U.S., but only up to high school. She speaks English very well. She didn't want to continue studying. She is probably sleeping right now. What time is it right now? Is it 1:00 in the afternoon? She's still in bed right now. She attended high school and didn't want to study anymore. She wanted to work in a salon. She went to school in a beauty salon - it cost $12,000, for one year. To finally finish the course, she had to go live in Southern California. It was the last assignment, and she didn't do it. She did not get a certificate, and the money, I had to pay $12,000, was wasted. Because if you do not have the certificate, what do you have? Nothing, really.

"Then Alicia started going to people's homes to do odd jobs, and nothing else. She then started to work in San José, in security for a company called Sysco. She worked for 5 years there, at night. But one day they found her sleeping, and they told her not to sleep on the job. Another day, they found her sleeping again, and they told her that it is work, not sleep. The third time, bye, they fired her. Now she's got nothing. And she's not looking, because she says she won't until her unemployment runs out. I told her, 'Look honey you drive, you're young; you can get a job anywhere. You are 24 years old and know English and Spanish.' But she's not looking, she isn't looking. She doesn't want to work, because she's very comfortable. I tell her to get a job in whatever she has experience. Her mom bought her a car and it cost $14,000. It's not a new car. She asked for the car and asked, and asked. Well, after a lot of insistence my wife said, 'I'll buy her a cheap car.' She bought it and gave it to her. She got a license soon after that, and that's when she went to work for the security company. She just doesn't want to work. It is a problem.

"Alicia also has a son, Eli, three years old. And who knows where the father is. Eli lives with us, but he doesn't go to school, yet, he's too young. He speaks English. My daughter tells us not to talk to him in Spanish, but since I do not know English, I always speak Spanish. And my wife speaks English to him, so the kid barely knows any Spanish, hardly anything.

"In my family, I am the one's who's economically less. My brothers and sisters are working, doing great things. There is a brother who does bridge construction, by contract, and has a great job. My other brother can do that, but no longer wants to work in the sun so now he makes bathrooms, inside, but he makes good money, because it's by contract. Another brother lives in Seattle. He learned how to draw in Mexico. At first he painted players' shirts and then he worked in Mexico for Banamex, the National Bank of Mexico and Pemex, the state owned petroleum company, drawing pictures – making plans for roads. He is in Seattle right now. He moved to Seattle from San Francisco and right now he works at universities, doing painting and drawing. He also paints on cars. He has a very good job, but what he doesn't have is money. Because he spends it all, he spends it all.

"Out of nine children, there are eight of us left, five men and three women. My sister would have been 72 right now, two years in between, my following brother is 70, a sister is 68, another brother 66, then there's me at 64 and two by two to finish 9! Only the first one died, – she was walking and fell, from heart failure. The doctor told her one day, 'You are ill, I can see a spot in your heart and you will die quickly, you will not suffer.' She was told that she would die quickly and she did, she did not suffer.

"It was many years before I came to the Day Worker Center. I had been in the States 30 years when I came here. This center has been in many places. I first saw it when it was on El Camino Real, near Walmart. I watched as the workers entered, but I never entered. I watched as I passed. From there they moved to California Avenue. I walked in front of it many times, but I never entered. I started coming to the Center when it was on Mercy St., near Castro St. in Mountain. View. I had worked in a carpentry company, Harmon Construction, beginning in 1995, for 12 years, building houses. Then I stopped working there and I came to the Day Worker Center. We moved to the new Center on Escuela Avenue three years ago.

"What I like to do most is digging, because before I worked in a carpentry company, I worked for 12 years in a company doing excavations for foundations. That's where I made more money - that is where I made the most. In the Day Worker Center there are fewer options, only jobs like moving, painting, or gardening. That is what's most abundant here. Yes, I like it; it beats having nothing. It's better. Now I work possibly four or five days a week - even more, sometimes. Four days for sure, whole days. Yes, many employers call me. On Monday, I worked 8 hours, on Tuesday I did not work because I went to the clinic, but I worked yesterday for eight hours. I work almost every day.

"Every day after work I go to see volleyball in the park. But I don't go with Esther. Volleyball, it's fun. It amuses me and affects me a little, because I bet and I lose. $20, $40, $60. Sometimes I win and sometimes I lose, but I lose more than what I win. On Saturday, I won about $40, but lost $60 on Sunday! So no, it is not a good business. Eventually, I'll stop working. But I'm never home. I go outside and spend time walking around. Because if there are no people in the house I do not like being there alone and if there are people in the house I don't like it either, so I'm not very adept. Sometimes, I come to the Day Worker Center at half past 6 in the morning, 6:20 to 6:30. Sometimes, if I am not at work at two in the afternoon, I stay until 5:00 and then I go out to San Jose to watch the volleyball game. I arrive home at 9:00 p.m. I leave early and arrive late.

"I often go to Mexico – I have gone many times by bus and plane. I have an ID and a green card, but I could not get a driver's license. I have been on planes, but I do not like it, I am scared of flying. I do not like it, but I've done it. When my father died I flew home; when my mom had surgery for the first time, too. Three times I've flown, but I went by plane and returned by bus. About two years ago, the director of the Day Worker Center and several of the workers went to Washington D.C. for immigration reform. I was invited, but I didn't want to go. I don't like airplanes.

"But I'll stay here in the U.S permanently. I have no capital, neither here nor there. Being poor there or being poor here, it's better here. But I am happy I came. I only want to go to Mexico for three weeks and then return – that is what I want. I'm going to apply for U.S. citizenship. After five years of being a resident, a person can be a citizen. I haven't done it before, well just because you say, 'Tomorrow, tomorrow, tomorrow.' I will have to take the exam. It's not hard. It is difficult, but only because I do not know English. But at my age I can take it in Spanish. Fifty-five years or more, you can take it in Spanish, so for me it is not hard. I just leave it for tomorrow, tomorrow, and tomorrow.

"What I want out of life is to work eight hours, five days a week, a steady job, not six or seven or ten hours a day, no, just eight hours and five days. Simple, nothing else. I also want good health, and to have no enemies. I don't have any now, but I wouldn't want to, ever. My dad told us to try to live well, not be spiteful, that if ever a person insulted us, not to mind. It'll pass; it will pass, because if one pays attention to every little problem one would always have problems. If someone walked by me and was drunk and pushed me and insulted me? Ah, don't mind, don't mind. Others go for the gun and they find each other and kill each other. I've seen things like that. So if one paid attention to all these little things we'd already be six feet under. We'd be in prison; we'd have lost an eye from a punch. It's better to be a bit of a coward than a little bit brave, because in Mexico there is all of that violence all the time. Your brother killed my brother, I seek your brother and I don't find him, but I find you, pum, pum, pum, only because your brother killed my brother and that should not be, it should not be. That happens a lot in Mexico – revenge. Families are killed. It's horrible.

"Now I'm healthy. I'm not missing an eye. I'm not missing a hand, a foot. And what else… Who knows? So hopefully my daughter will find a job tomorrow. She says she'll find one and work, but she says that every day, but she is not looking for it. I pay taxes every year. But, I do not know if I can retire now, because if I do not keep putting money into social security, it won't increase anymore. If you give me $5 right now for retirement, if I don't work it's going to be the same, it will not grow, right? And I am ready to apply for retirement, because I am 64.

"When one gets older I feel everything closes up a bit. I'm going to be walking around dragging a foot and maybe with a blind eye; I feel like I'll get to that. Because I don't know how long I will last. But you never know in life, will it be 20, will it be 30, will it be 2 will it be 1, or tomorrow we don't know, but I do not analyze it.

"Life has taught me many things. I have gotten to know many things, good and bad, because life shows you everything. It was all good, because I never, when I was here or there, or young or old, have fought with another person. If anyone ever throws a punch at me they will break my jaw because I know nothing. So that's why I have not had bad experiences. I have learned not to fight. That's what I learned, a good point. Look I trust everyone. We live better when we trust. I'd like to be remembered as good people."

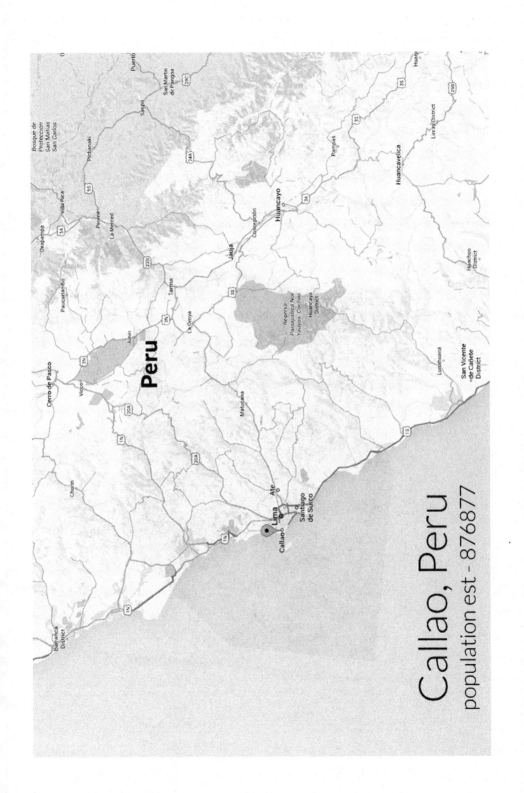

Callao, Peru
population est - 876877

Chapter 2

Ernesto's Story

"It is a bad time in my life, a difficult time. Because right now I do not have documents to work and, indeed, I am illegal in the United States. My visa expired, because I entered legally on a tourist visa and stayed. I overstayed. And I cannot get a job that matches my skills and my education.

"I'm from Callao, Peru. That is the port of Lima. My journey has been from Peru, to Japan and finally the United States. Why Japan? Because in the 1990's - in 1992 or 1993, the situation in Peru was very critical. There was so much terrorism and the terrorist group 'Sendero Luminoso' (Shining Path) was a Maoist insurgent organization that had surrounded Lima. It was a civil war – they were trying to establish a dictatorship of the proletariat. It was a brutal organization and used violence against peasants, trade unions, elected officials and the general civilian population. We all knew people that had been killed by violence and bombs. It was a very dangerous country in those years, but there was also the opportunity to travel by visa to Japan. The president of Peru was a descendant of Japan and so the two countries had a relationship. Also, at that time, Japan had a need for a lot of workers. So I decided to leave Peru.

"I was born on 26 March, 1953. I am old - 61 years old. My dad is also named Ernesto. I do not like my middle name - Braulio. It comes from a saint. At the time that I was born it was common to use names from the calendar. My dad was born in Lima, itself. My mom was born north of Lima, in another department - Chimbote, which is a fishing port. My mom came from the countryside. My father was a city man, who hated countrymen. You know the term 'Indians.' Well, in Peru, you call them 'Cholos'. Cholos in Mexico is another thing. In Mexico cholo is a gang member. In South America, Cholo is Indian, dismissive. 'That Cholo crap!' My mom always told me that my dad was mean to her. Sometimes, he would say 'Hey, Chola ...' and you know, they had fights.

"My grandparents were Italian and Spanish and came to Peru. At that time it was difficult to live in Europe because of the war, the famine. I did not know them. They died before I was born. My father and my mother were both orphaned when they were children. So I do not know what it is to have grandparents. My dad was raised by his grandfather, and my mother by her older siblings. She was the youngest of the siblings.

"My dad was white. He was the son of Italians and had light eyes, lighter than mine and he looked a lot more 'gringo', whiter than me, you could say, so he felt entitled. There is racism in our countries. I look just like my dad, but my dad was whiter. In terms of personality it's a bit complicated. I sometimes say I am becoming more and more like my dad, because I like drinking. My father drank in the street and he would call me. 'Son! Son! Come and see!' I would hide. I think in that way I had a traumatic relationship with my dad.

"My mother separated from my father when I was three years old. Well, as I said, the first three years of my life we lived in Callao. My father was a merchant and the port was there. He collected the merchandise that was imported from everywhere. I lived there until I was three. We lived in a home, but my parents sold it later. There were three bedrooms, living room, and kitchen. A normal house - two bathrooms as well.

"From there we went to live in Lima. It's not a long trip - twenty minutes. We began to live in a rented house. I was living with my mom and my two siblings – my older sister, and my younger brother.

"I almost do not remember Callao, as I was only three when we left. Lima is a cosmopolitan, big city. Similar to Mexico City. It has 10 million inhabitants. I lived in the midst of the city, in the concrete jungle. I have never lived in the countryside. I do not even like the countryside. Well, maybe for a day, to walk a little, but then I get bored and mosquitoes start biting and I just return to the city.

"My mom did not work. My father never paid alimony to my mom. When they got divorced, my mom said it was very hard. She had a little savings here and there. He just went away. My dad went to the United States - to San Francisco. A few years later, he returned to Lima. He said he missed his children, his three children. But when he returned he had a drinking problem. He lost his business and everything else. I do not remember him from when I was a kid. I remember him as an older man, when he approached us apologetically. I do not resent him. I even buried him.

"When I was ten or so, my mom remarried. My stepfather was a United States police colonel. She created another home and we lived with him in Lima. I called my stepfather 'dad'. He brought us up practically. My mom and stepfather had a son - my stepbrother – who now lives in the United States. He is a U.S. citizen, because his dad was from the U.S.

"In my youth I got in trouble. I had a crazy youth. In the 1970's, I was a hippie. Long hair and drugs. Yes, I had problems; do I have to tell you? I don't need to hide it from you, I smoked marijuana as a boy. It was illegal, of course. My mom would pick me up from the police station. Eventually, I went to school and I calmed down. My brother, however, was more serious. I'm the black sheep of the family.

"I went to college, at the Metropolitan Higher Institute of Lima, where I learned technical drawing. It is a technical degree, a career in middle management. In the Metropolitan Higher Institute of Lima I did two years of drawing and then became a civil construction technician. It applies to a very wide range of jobs, to be a helper of a civil engineer. His right hand, like a master builder.

"When I was twenty years old, I taught. I volunteered in the church and taught literacy to people who could not read back in my country. And I liked it. I taught writing, everything. I like teaching. I like to teach many people. Sometimes, now, I will correct when some colleagues say an incorrect word; then I correct them. I teach them real Spanish, Castilian, which is what we speak.

"I didn't serve in the military. It was mandatory at that time. I went and, as I was a bit shortsighted, I said, 'I'm blind, I cannot see.' 'Okay, go over there.' I was exonerated. It was quite easy. At that time they sought you. There were raids to find young people to get them by force to join the army.

"I married at age 20. I got a girl pregnant when I was 20 years old. Precisely at that time I stopped partying a bit and I had to work. I really wanted to apply to the Faculty of Architecture, which was what I liked. I couldn't continue my studies because I had to start working as an engineer. She was really young, too. We got married in Peru, in Lima. We got married in a church. She was, you would not believe this, 15 years old. And her dad was a cop. In the United States they put you in jail for something like that. In Peru, you get a choice: you have to marry or go to jail. Anyway, that was the hardest time of my life. I had to work and my aspirations for a career in architecture or civil engineering were gone. From then on, I've been working my entire life.

"I had already worked in the construction company, drawing plans for architecture and construction for about 20 years when I decided to leave for Japan. By then, I had divorced my first wife. A few years before I decided to leave for Japan, the construction company I worked for sent me to work in Cuzco, Peru. Machu Picchu is there. I went there to work on the renovations of a hotel, the best hotel in Cuzco at the time, a tourist hotel. There I met my second wife Anabella. My second wife is from Cuzco. I stole her away and brought her with me to Lima, where we got married. A few years went by, four years, but we had no children. We still didn't have any children by the time we left Lima to go to Japan. I thought one of us might have problems, might be infertile, that we couldn't conceive. We came to Japan and she became pregnant. I do not know what happened, maybe the climate change, I do not know. It must be the change in hemisphere. Anabella was very young. I was already 34 and she was 20. There we had a child - my daughter - who is now 20 years old.

"We lived in Japan for 14 years. My daughter was born there, she speaks Japanese, and she behaves like all Japanese. She also speaks perfect Spanish, because we spoke to her in Spanish, but she is Japanese. She lives there with her mom.

"Living in Japan was very difficult at first. In the first year, second year, I suffered a lot. To communicate I had to sign a lot. Sometimes you were told 'You're a fool' and you didn't even realize. You would have said 'arigato, arigato, sayonara' and they were saying, 'You are stupid,' 'arigato, sayonara.' Eventually I learned to speak a little Japanese. I'll tell you one thing, the one thing that happens in Japan is that the Japanese are not very friendly to you. They are not rude or angry, they don't resent you; they are scared of you. If you talk to them in English, they are scared of you. Furthermore, when they have a few drinks and want to talk to you, you can say you're Chinese or Spanish but they will believe that you speak English. They always believe that the foreign language is English - it's amazing. But the Japanese do not speak English, they don't know how to speak English, they are afraid of English. The only place where English is spoken is at the counters at the international airport. It's the only place. Not like here.

"In Japan, I had two different jobs, the first with auto parts. I worked for two years in a factory. Auto parts from that factory were exported all over the world to the United States from Toyota, Nissan. Japanese cars are all pretty much the same; they have nothing different from each other. If you check your car, Toyota has the same piece, a capacitor or whatever, it has the same piece as a Nissan, Mazda, that is, the car is standard, and there is no car that is better than the other. Now, it may be better because of the engine or the power, but no worse or better in quality. You can never say that a Toyota is better quality because they are the same parts; it's the same factory. In the factory, I worked in the press making tubes for air conditioning on cars. Everything there is machine controlled. I have also gone to the factories where they make the cars themselves. For example there are doors, doors, doors, shelves, chassis, chassis, and chassis. What a rich country, I really miss that country. In the U.S. there are car factories, but they are far away. I think cars are made in Detroit in the United States.

"From there I went to work at a paper mill company. They made countless types of paper. We made giant spools of two tons of paper. From there, they then send the spools to another site, where they cut it and make it into legal size, and other sizes of paper. I drove a forklift. When the warm paper came out, something like a giant two-ton or three-ton spool, I came with the forklift. It was a special forklift. And you know who would throw the paper? A robot. A giant robot labeled the paper, everything. I grabbed the spool, and you had to have great technique, because if you grabbed it in the wrong way, some of the paper would be ruined. A small mistake could scrap some 100 layers of paper and they would have to be sent to recycling. The paper was worth hundreds of dollars. It was hard, but sometimes I even did it when I was sleepy, or drunk, it was an automated thing.

"In Japan I made $3000 - $ 4000 per month. I could even afford to have three girlfriends! I was a 40 year-old man in the prime of my life. There were plenty of women there that were not Japanese - Russian, Romanian, Ukrainian, Eastern European, blondes with blue eyes, as well. You didn't even look at the Japanese. What's more, if you like brunettes more – there were women from the Philippines up for grabs. It is very difficult for Japanese women to accept you, and for the family to accept you and for her to consider you as a boyfriend.

"I was a womanizer. I would go out all the time in my car. My wife got tired, and me, too. Then we split up. I started living alone in Japan when I separated from my wife. I felt alone and I used to go clubbing. I knew all the discos in Japan. In Japan there is a building, and it's so well done that you see a door that looks like a flat, open the door and it's a nightclub, another door, another nightclub. Licensed, everything. Japan's nightlife is incredible, it's unbelievable. I've never seen anything like it. Many things are legal there. I'm not going to lie.

"We spent a few years separated like that. She took my daughter, but we lived near each other. I didn't miss anything. My daughter's school was close to my house. If she wanted to come to my house, she had a key to my little apartment, and she came and opened the door. 'Hello daddy, hello, hello.' We were like friends.

"But the time came when I had to renew my visa - there are no permanent visas in Japan. There are permanent visas, but not like here, where you have the green card and you're done. Over there you renew it every three years. I went to the immigration office to renew my Japanese visa. I knew what was going to happen. They asked: 'Where is your wife?' 'She is not here.' 'She has to come.' 'Why?' Because my wife was giving me the visa - she was a Japanese descendant and she was giving me the visa. They said, 'Oh, no, but the wife has to come.' 'But I am divorced and I have a child that was born here.' 'Yeah, that's fine, but hey, I'm sorry, sayonara!'

"I regret the madness. I regret what I did in Japan. I mean, going out with women and stuff. I lost my home and my wife. Yes that's the saddest thing. Because she's a good woman. She got married again, to a Japanese man.

"I cannot go back to Japan. I cannot go back because immigration laws are very strict there. I was told to leave. I wasn't expelled, that's good; if not, I would not have been able to enter the United States. And Japan's foreign policy remains the same. The border is even more closed. They no longer accept immigration, not even if I am the Peruvian son of Fujimori, the former president.

"Since I could not stay in Japan, I called my nephew in California and said, 'Hey I have problems with Anabella.' He knew that we had separated. The problem is that immigration is asking me where my wife is, but I have no wife and then I will not be able to renew my visa. You have to be careful, because Japan is a very dangerous place to go without a visa, because police in Japan ask for documents at any time of the day. Also, I had become bored with Japan - too much partying.

"My nephew, who is a U.S. citizen, is the son of my sister. He is an architect by profession, but is not practicing right now. He practiced in Peru. In the U.S. he has a job that has nothing to do with architecture, in one of those medical technology companies. He said, 'Come here uncle, here's the place to be. We'll make it.' In the end I came to the U.S. and everything was just talk. 'No, uncle, the thing is, employment is low, wait;

be patient.' I arrived just when the economic crisis hit the US. There were no jobs, no work in 2008.

"I came to the United States on a tourist visa from Japan. I stayed with my nephew, who lived in Palo Alto, California. He said, 'Yes, uncle, don't worry uncle, we'll make it.' I came with some savings, about $ 4000. I spent six months not working. Then the money ran out. But I was lucky - I met a friend who introduced me to someone who said, 'Hey! There is the Day Worker Center where you can get work.' But wait, I went to the Center, hanging around, but nothing happened. After about three months I went to Utah to see my stepbrother, who is married to an American. Then I spent a year in Utah in Salt Lake City. Everywhere pure snow - how awful!

"I worked in Utah eventually, but the worst was that there was practically no work and the weather was horrible. Horrible. In California you may not have a job, but here you are with friends, there's sun, vegetation. There, it's horrible - and there are only Mormons. Utah is the state of the Mormons, it's a state created for them. Everyone is a Mormon. My brother is a Mormon.

"My family has not helped me. My older sister married an American and she'll become a citizen, too, one of these days. She has not submitted any papers for me yet. She has not submitted a single request for my green card or anything. She says, 'Ahh, but wait! Do you have the money?' Because you have to go pay a fine, something for forgiveness, I am not sure what it is.

"It was the same thing with my brother who lives in Utah - the son of my stepfather. My mom is living in his house and is 82 years old. She talks to me every day. She will become a citizen also. Because she's been here for five years and is over 70 years old, she is not asked to know English. Showing that your child is a citizen is all you need. And she can request it for me, if she doesn't die before that, poor thing.

"From my mom and dad we are my sister, then me, and my recently deceased brother. He died at 56 or 57 years old. He was a professional public accountant. His daughters had a great education, one is an industrial engineer, and the other one studied business administration. He lived in Peru. My brother traveled around the world for conferences. He went to India, to England. He was the chief auditor. Auditors are accountants, well, a certain specialty job for accountants. He traveled the world and seemed well positioned; he had a home and everything, and he had a heart attack. Younger than me. He was my younger brother by one year and died at 59. We had even studied at school as if we were twins as young children, in the same school year. We celebrated birthdays together, just to save a bit on the party. Our birthdays were only one week apart. We'd celebrate on a Sunday with cake and all. Our cousins would come. Those are beautiful memories.

"My son by my first wife is now 40 years old and lives with his mother in Canada. He is a Canadian citizen. They live in Quebec, Montreal and speak French. Their children also can speak Spanish, because at home they speak Spanish. Now I get along well with my first wife, the mother of my son. My son went to law school and became a lawyer. He studied in Peru when he lived there, but when he arrived in Canada, he was told he would have to go back to school to practice. He decided not to study in Canada, and so he does not practice the profession. My boy already has his life - he has given me three grandchildren, he is married, and just bought a house in Canada. He said that there is a room for me for when I decide to go. He wanted me to go and live there. But I wouldn't get used to it and I do not want to bother them. I don't want to be a burden. They say it is terribly cold there, 20 degrees below zero in the winter; the pool freezes. It's horrible. I like California. I think it's the best climate in the world.

"My daughter is 20 years old and lives in Japan with her mother. My daughter speaks Spanish and Japanese. But I cannot decipher her Facebook page. She doesn't want to be my friend on Facebook, but I can see her photos and she'll write in Japanese, so I cannot understand. I sent her a friend request, but she does not want to be my friend.

"My daughter is a problem. She's young and I wanted her to go to continue with school. She was studying languages. But now she has started to work and stopped going to college. She bought a car. In Japan anyone can afford a car. It's like here, too, all the sons of Americans have their own cars. She bought the car with her salary, go figure. In Japan, a girl of 14 or 15 years if they already have more or less a certain body height can be given permission to work. They work in cell factories or things of that sort.

"About four years ago, I went to the Day Worker Center. It has helped me a lot — helped me to survive. Now I do the simplest work - a bit of carpentry, gardening. I don't like to paint, I hate painting! Every time I have started to paint, I lost my jeans or spoiled my clothes. We get to the center 'Come! Ernesto! You are leaving! You have to go to work! You're going to paint this,' and I did not bring the right clothes. I am not a professional painter. You end up painting yourself. I have to keep working until I get tired. I have no social security here. There are people at the Day Worker Center who are nearly 70 years old and continue to work, and come here. It is heavy work. It can be shoveling, moving.

"Right now, I work part time in a warehouse of Moroccan handicrafts. I earn $15 per hours and I work three times a week, for eight hours – 24 hours a week. I do many things – I store, I pack, unpack. The warehouse is very big, and it has big shelving full of products, lamps. It is called Casablanca Market. It had a shop on Castro Street in Mt. View, but now I do not know where they are selling. The owners hired me from the Day Worker Center. They went to the Center and looked for a person to help them, and then another person, and another one; but the lady was very particular. She did not put up with them. 'OK, bring another, bring another,' until I went and she liked me and I have been working there for a year and a half. And I speak a little English, because the others did not speak any English. The owners say, 'Do this' and the other workers would go to sleep. They know that I am not here legally. However, the owner likes how I work. I get paid in cash – outside of the books.

"I've had false papers, but now I don't have them. I think only 5% of the people have false documents. I have been offered fake IDs, - but no, – I do not want to do those things. I've had a California driver's license, but it's expired. The police stopped me twice while driving and the fine for each ticket was $472. So from that day on I had no car. I don't want to be working just to pay the DMV, so I do not drive anymore. I don't have any social security. To find work I go to the Day Worker Center. You are waking up to the reality here. I've never had a problem with the law here. Especially since I do not look like an immigrant. There once was a raid and I watched how they took Mexicans away, but to me they said nothing, not even the time of day.

"I am very outgoing and I know many people from many countries. I worked 14 years with Brazilians. I speak Portuguese. I have worked with Filipinos, with Japanese. Now, from time to time, with Americans, Moroccans, with Hindus who constantly go to the Center to request a worker. They all like me. Sometimes I hear the other men say, 'Ernesto always has help from the office.' They say that every day I go to work. But sometimes people come and, for example, nobody wants to work with

Hindus. They say 'No, that does not pay well,' but to me, Ernesto, they come to get me, calling me directly on my phone, to work. 'Hey, why do Hindus always ask for you? You get sent by the office, right? 'No!' 'It's one thing in which I differentiate from the others. These men, Mexicans, Central Americans, think that it's about being strong, but they do not speak, do not have the gift of conversation. When I go to work with employers I start to talk in English. I say, 'I'm from Peru. Where are you from?' 'Then,' 'Ah! Yes! Peru? Machu Picchu!' And so I don't get heavy work and they become my friends. Now I work almost every day, and the rest of the men do not. They have a different mentality. So I think my gift is to be outgoing with people of all cultures.

"No, sometimes people don't like me - they think I'm a smartass. That I act like I know a lot. But I think I have a certain level of culture. Of culture, not of intelligence - I'm talking culture. I know many things, many people. I think that's my strength and I think that's what happens with employers. Employers call me back. 'Ernesto, come!' And there have been employers who have gone to find me at the Center and I was not there and do you think they took another worker? 'Oh no, tell him to see if he can come on Saturday. I'll come back on Saturday to see if he can come, or whenever he can.' Or they'll call me. They have my number and everything. Which does not happen with others there in the center.

"No one gives me a job just like that. They give me work because, as I said, they know me and have taken a liking. But just imagine if it ends. Do you know what the problem is, too? In winter, the work in the Day Worker Center is low; it slows a lot. People go to work once a week, once a week. How can you live on $ 100 a week?

"Now I rent a room in a house in Mt. View. It is a home owned by a Mexican family and I rent a room. Five people live in the house. There is another room that is also rented. Before I was renting alone, $700 just for a room. But I had to get a roommate, because the bills went up. I met my roommate at the Center. Bernardo is from Chile. He no longer comes to the Center these days. He works elsewhere. He comes to the Center occasionally, but when he gets a job, he usually works for a month. He is a good carpenter, a house carpenter. Not furniture. Because in our country the carpenter makes furniture, but here a carpenter makes frames for houses. Yes, in Peru houses are built with brick, concrete.

"When I am not working I go to a club around here on Castro Street in Mt. View. I go with my Mexican friend Daniel to the disco. I go drinking with my friends. I go to San Francisco and go to a restaurant with my family in Palo Alto. I also play the guitar. We have a group at the Day Worker Center and sometimes we perform in the local communities or restaurants. We play for tips.

"I've reached a ceiling. I'm hoping to retire. I'm going to officially retire in Japan, and they'll send money to me here. I already got an advance. It was three years ago, I was sent a check, and I'll receive a Japanese pension, because I worked more than 14 years in that country. So I contributed, paid taxes; they deducted 25% of what I earned. If you earn $4000 almost $1000 went for retirement. And I always had good health care. When I got sick, I received the best medical care in hospitals. While I was in Japan, I had back problems. By doing nothing. I do not know why I had this problem. Maybe by being on the lift, the movement, the discs of the vertebrae became damaged, and I gained weight. Because the work was actually easy. When there was no production left, the boss would tell us to go for coffee, rest.

"I could go back to Peru, if I get papers in the United States. But the truth is that since my brother died, I have no family there. That's another thing, there are people who tell me 'Hey! Buy a car!' No! I do not want to get a fine and I want to have a clear record, enough with the expired license. 'No! But what?' 'You know who tells me that?' Those people who do not mind having fines, or do not care, because they are sending money home and then plan to stay in their own countries. In their country they are building their houses. I have to be more careful. I have to watch myself because I want my bones buried here, to be buried here.

"I want a dignified old age. Not like some people older than me that are at the Center. I would like a decent old age, perhaps working in a softer job. I aspire not to make a lot of money, but as I say, a dignified old age. Working perhaps as a clerk in a store, something such as Fry's Electronics, so to speak. Something to be in contact with people. But I have to improve my English.

"Most importantly, I want to meet a mature woman and get married. Because I had a child at 20, my second daughter at 40, and I'm 60 now and I need a third wife. Marrying for the company and also the papers, too. Why should I be a hypocrite? Because even if my sister asks for a green card for me, or my brother asks for a green card for me, until I get the green card it will be at least 15 years. Instead, with a marriage to a

U.S. citizen, in three years, No! In six months you have a green card and in three years you can be a citizen. That's how it works here.

"So I'm looking for a girlfriend. I have a special friend – Ludmila - but it's nothing official. A friend with benefits. She is a Russian-American and lives in Saratoga. She has been here for 10 or 15 years. I met her at a barbecue. She is about 63 years old. She was a teacher in Russia. She is Jewish and Jews get visas to enter and before long, become citizens. It's like the Cubans - it is almost impossible to find a Cuban illegal. Because when a Cuban is on American soil, in a month they give them a green card.

"The government - I do not know how it's done - but the government pays Ludmila - gives her an apartment. I do not know why the government helped her for being Jewish. Policy. It is as if she has political asylum, but that was then. This is not the era of Stalin. What happens is that it is a political issue. Why help the Jews? Why do Americans give weapons to the Jews? Give logistical support? But that's another problem, they do not want to see it. Hitler died, Stalin died and why do the Jews need so much help? But it's very easy, very easy. Because, basically, all it is a political issue. Why for the Latinos, is it not easy and it is easy for others? They come from Russia, Ukraine, even countries like Pakistan, India, because it is a political game. The United States is not interested in Latinos. If you go to Mountain View, it is the same - pure Chinese, because here they get a visa easily.

"I wanted to marry Ludmila out of convenience. She is my official girlfriend - I introduced her to everyone, and she knows my family. I introduced her to my brothers and even to my mom when she came to visit me. So you can say that she was my official girlfriend. She also wanted to get married, but the problem is that when I asked her to marry me she went to find out about our situation.

"She went to city hall and she learned she would lose some benefits by marriage and said, 'No, let's go on like this.' She didn't leave me, but said, 'Let's live together, but we cannot get married, because the government will take my pension, will take this, take that, and my apartment will become more expensive.' She even gets paid retirement. They would reduce it. She receives a check for $900 monthly. If she married me she would no longer receive the $900. Her brother said, 'Ah, you want to marry this man? He should provide for you.' She worked in the U.S. for only five years and paid taxes. Americans do not know these things because they are never interested in knowing. It's like they live in another world.

"If I do not marry Ludmila, I will try and find another woman to marry. I keep both options in mind. Now I have a new girlfriend – Lucia. She is a friend - a good friend. I met her in Mountain View. I was walking with a friend and he introduced us. Even though I am old, I have some social activity. She is also working - she is Mexican. But I have no interest in getting married, because she does not have a green card. She is in the same situation as me, but right now she is legal, here with a tourist visa, comes and goes, comes and goes.

"I am an old man. That's the uncertainty that I have. Suddenly, I'm too old, I'm not going to get anything, and I will not get a partner. Suddenly, I do not know, I could get a heart attack. That's my insecurity, that's what worries me. Well, you learn from your mistakes, too, I'm going to say. There are things that can no longer be undone. It's already done. But it leaves a mark. But one learns."

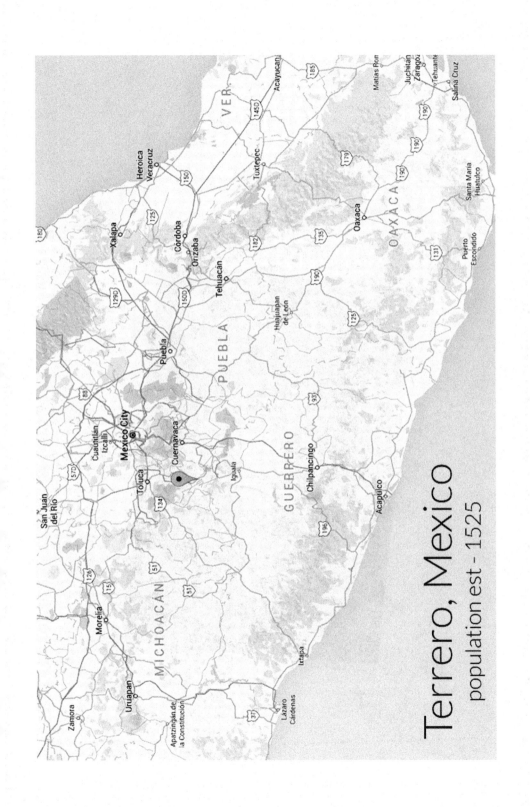

Terrero, Mexico
population est - 1525

Chapter 3

Lucía's Story

"I was born in Mexico, in 1965, in Terrero, a town about two and a half hours south of Mexico City. I lived in a tile house in the very center of the village; everything was close. About three blocks away there was the church, opposite that the government building, across from that was the bank, on the other block were many restaurants.

"We lived in our own house. My father told us that when he planted onions, he would sell them and when he did well, he used the money to buy the land and gradually built the house. We only had two rooms and a kitchen and a corridor. We had no bathroom. We had a space in the back yard that we called a 'corral' where my dad had a horse and he had chickens. My dad never let his daughters ride the horse - only my brothers. I remember that although at first we were allowed to keep animals, at some point it was forbidden. Once, you could have pigs, but then you no longer could. So my father had to move his horse; he took it away, up on a hill. He had some land there; he put up a roof for protection, and that's where he left his horse.

"My mother worked in the house. She was always at home, taking care of us. She was very dedicated, I remember when I was younger, I didn't have to do anything. Only my oldest sister used to help out, she'd make tortillas, she'd do groceries. My other sister too, one would wash and the other would iron, and so on. They'd distribute the work between them.

"My father worked mainly as a day worker, as his father had done. He usually worked by seasons. During the rainy season he'd plant crops. He grew corn, planted onions. Our family earned money only by my father's jobs. We never went hungry, but my parents could not buy many needed things for us.

"My grandparents were also born in Terrero. I remember my grandfather; we called him *abuelito*, my mother's father. He dedicated himself to doing this thing called *chiquihuites*; by weaving reeds and *otate* he made some type of baskets, squared and round ones. People bought them; they were called *tapaderas*. A cloth was placed on them and then they were meant to store tortillas. My grandmother, his wife, stayed at home. Sometimes, she also helped him in that she would sweep the streets of people that would ask her and then paid her. She also helped make meals - it was not a restaurant, it was called a *fonda*, she'd go there to grind chili in a mill. She was a good cook.

"My mother had two children that died when they were babies. One came after my brother Javier. My mom said he caught some kind of cough. *Tos hogona* is what they called it at the time and he died. I guess, I think it would have been bronchitis, or something like that. But back then my mom used to say that he died of *tos hogona*. It was when children caught a bad cough and couldn't stop coughing. She told me he was about a year old. I never met him.

"Then after me another girl was born, but she died. She didn't die during the pregnancy; she got to the end of the pregnancy. I do not know if she was born sick and then died or if she was actually stillborn.

"In all, I have three sisters and six brothers. I am the sixth sibling – two brothers live in Minneapolis, I live in California and the rest live in Mexico. I haven't seen my siblings since I've moved to the United States. But we talk over the phone. Sometimes I send them some money, but not always. I only send money when someone is ill. Right now, one sister is sick with diabetes. She's sick, and her husband is a day worker in Mexico. I do not know how much they pay him right now, maybe 120 or 150 pesos per day. He is only a day worker and there are times when it rains, there are times when there's no work. There is more work is the rainy season, when many people want to plant. But sometimes, if it rains too much, there is no work.

"All my brothers and sisters and also my cousins liked to go play together outside at the side of our house. We played there in the afternoon when there weren't many cars on the street. We liked to play with different things and different games. It is not like now - with smartphones and video games. No. Playing hide and seek, 'the black man,' 'the birds,' and 'the onions.' When we played the birds we gathered a lot of children. One would sell birds and the other bought them and the one selling had all the kids lined up and would give each person a special name, a name or a color. Then when the buyer came he would ask, 'Can you sell me a bird?' 'What color?' And he would say, 'Green' 'No, no, there are no green left' so then he'd say, 'Blue' 'Oh! This one is blue.' And 'How much does it cost?' The buyer would pay him and the bird would run away and the buyer would have to catch him; if he didn't it was no longer his.

"When I turned twelve, I helped out in the house, too. I had to sweep the kitchen or the street. Every day we would sweep out the side of the street from the house. I went to school, too. My parents would only send me to primary school. After going to school, I helped my mom in the house. I wanted to learn to knit, because some ladies in the village, some women, came together to weave thread, called estambrón. My sisters also knitted; they got paid for the work they did. They made shawls, but shaped like triangles. I learned how to knit, a little, but since then I've forgotten how to do it. Well that's what I did, nothing else, knitting. We would knit all week and on Saturday we had to deliver what we did.

"My school was quite a big school and after I left they remodeled it and made it larger. There were several grades, many first and second grade classes. I was walking distance from school - close by. It was about two blocks away. I lived close to most things in the neighborhood. The market, church, bank, office, and school.

"I finished my sixth year in school. It was the neighborhood school. I was more or less a good student. I would get eights out of ten. You could pass with a six, but you were barely making it through then. What I liked most was Spanish – language class.

"I wanted to be a nurse, but never studied it. I always think about that - I did not know why my parents were that way. That is why I tell my children, 'Study, here you have the opportunity to study.' I encourage them to make an effort and continue studying. Because they have opportunities to study, and we did not get them, and would have liked to.

"My mom did not force us to continue studying. She didn't encourage us to go to school after primary school. When I was about 17 years, I told my mom I wanted to learn something else. In our town, situated next to the government building, was a special trade school. There, in that school, many courses were taught - there was sewing, making clothes, a knitting course and cooking classes. There was also a nursing course. You only had to pay before one entered - as a contribution or something - but it was not much and it was once, for the whole year. I told my mom, 'I am going to that school to study' and she said, 'No, you're not going anywhere.' 'Why?' 'Because all those women that say they are going to study just go to meet guys,' and she never allowed me to go. Back then one always obeyed their parents. When we were older, our father wouldn't even let us go out, he forbid it and said, 'No.' 'Where are you going? What will you do?' And just, 'No.' Sometimes, we left in secret and then when we got back, we got in trouble.

"My mom died in 1998 – the year before I came to the States. She got ill. She had a severe stomachache, and after a while her back started hurting, too. We took her to the doctor because it got to a point where it hurt just to walk. Wherever she was, if the pain started she'd have to sit down, and when it passed she could keep walking. She went to the doctor and got a few tests and x-rays. The doctor told her that she had a tumor, but said they were going to operate on it. She had the surgery, but they couldn't remove the tumor completely - it was already too large. When she had surgery, they only took a piece and that was sent for analysis to see what kind of tumor it was. They told us nothing came out. She remained like this for a while and when her back started hurting again my brother took her to the doctor. The doctor told my older brother and my sister and my other brother who died later, that she had no more options; that she would not heal. Then we did another x-ray and a shadow showed up in her lung, she had lung cancer. A month later, almost a month after that, she died.

"When my mother had passed and it was only my father in the house, he would give me money for household spending. I would cook and do everything. He'd give me money for the food. Also, my brother who stayed there, when his wife left him, lived there in the house. He'd work and between both of them they paid me. They gave me say fifty or sixty dollars and gave me half each. Then, when I wanted to buy soap I would tell them I needed money for soap, because I also washed and ironed for them. I would also work for others, if anyone would ask me to help out in their house or even wash or iron. I only cooked in our house.

"After my mom died, my dad did not want to be alone, so he was with another woman. He would leave on Fridays and would go to Taxco, a city where he would make a lot of money. He would go there to sell things, such as onions, cilantro, and carrots. He'd sell it all. He'd travel on Friday and return on Monday night or Tuesday morning, at about eight o'clock. While he was there, he was with another woman.

"And I was home with my brother. My brother who'd begun drinking daily and kept drinking and no longer worked. He was really lost. Then he got into AA and I was left alone in the house. My sister-in-law lived in the same house, but on the other side of the yard - because where the animal pen used to be, since we didn't have any animals left, they leveled the ground and made a small house for themselves.

"In 2002 my brother died. He drank a lot and he started suffering from cirrhosis. He recovered, but then was told he couldn't drink again. He lasted two or three years without having a drink, but then began to have a beer every once in a while... and so on. He got sick again and was in the hospital for about a month.

"My dad died in 2005. I was already here - in the States. He died because of all his drinking. He suffered from high blood pressure, because of the drinking. He didn't want to quit, maybe sometimes he'd quit for a few days and he did not drink a lot or only drank a beer. He did not understand he shouldn't drink at all and finally he got sick from it and started getting very slim and his belly got really big, it filled up with water. He was so sick and got admitted into the hospital. He got better and they'd discharge him, until one day they didn't.

"I thought about getting married. I was going to get married at about 28 years old, but I was a lot older when I got married. I used to think that I would get married and have children; for me it was nice to have children, but not too many. I thought that I'd have four tops, but I'd probably have three and I ended up having just two – two sons Leandro and Pablo.

"I met my future husband, Tomás, in Mexico, there, in my town. I met him because he was from Guerrero state. His family came to live in my village, where I lived. I did not know them very well. My husband's brother married my sister. After they got married I got to know them, and that's how we met. So they got married first. This happened long before we got together. We already knew each other but we were not together yet. We got to know each other in Mexico. After his father and mother died he left and came to the States in 1993 for a better life. I stayed in Mexico and we spoke on the phone. He kept saying he was going to return soon, but he did not. When he had been in the States for six years, he said he was returning to Mexico but that he was coming back to bring me to the States.

"Well I decided I wanted to come to the States because I always thought, 'I have to go to the U.S.; at least I have to visit it.' I was going to come with my brother but as my mother had died, only my dad was left. I asked my brother to help me come to the U.S., and he said, 'Yes, but with permission from my dad, you have to talk to him and if he gives you permission, then yes, I'll help you. If he says no, I cannot help you.' I talked to my dad then and he said, 'Yes, that he gave me permission.' I told my brother and my brother said, 'Tell him I want to talk to him, that this day I am going to come and talk to him.' I told my dad. When my brother was going to speak to him, I told my dad again, 'My brother wants to speak to you' and he said, 'You know what? I have said yes, but I already thought about it and you're not going anywhere.' He just refused. I was an adult - I was 34, but still he refused; he said, 'No and no.' And I asked him, 'But why not? Just for a few months nothing else! To get to know the country and come back.' 'No I told you you're not going to go anywhere, you will not treat me as if I'm clueless. You're going to go and you're not going to come back.'

"In 1999, I told my future husband, Tomás, I was coming to the U.S. and that I was going to come with my brother. My brother then said he would not help me, because my dad did not give me permission, so he was not going to help. I talked to Tomás and he said, 'OK, if you want to come I'll help you. Then I won't have to go over there to return with you, I can just save that money and help you come here. If you come then I'll help, I'll pay for all expenses and everything.'

"Then I got in touch with a person I knew was bringing people over to the U.S. I came with a man who brought people from our town over the border. It wasn't just me - there were many of us. There were 15 or 20 people from my town alone.

"I took a bag, a backpack with a change of clothes and money that was in my pocket in the inside of my pants. We traveled from my hometown to Mexico City by car, after that we took a plane in Mexico City to the border near Arizona. We crossed in Aguaprieta. That was not where the plane left us, I can't remember the name of that place, and we had a short drive to the border town. We did the whole trip in many small pieces. When we got there, we stayed one night. We got in late at night, so we stayed in a hotel that night and the next day, at six in the evening, or at seven, they picked us up and took us to a hill and we started walking to cross the border. At first we were 15 or 20 people, but then there on the hill many more came. We were like 30 in the end. We walked from 7:00 p.m. to 6:00 a.m. the next day. It was the month of October. It cost me $1,200. I had to pay extra.

"After we went over the hill we waited all day for someone to pick us up. Someone was supposed to pick us up and take us to Arizona. So we were there all day and we had nothing to eat, because we did not carry anything. We had a little bit of water, but by nighttime we had finished it. We no longer had water. At around 3:00 or 4:00 p.m., the person who guided us, communicated with another person, then this other person came and brought us a few gallons of water and some sandwich bread with mayonnaise – nothing else. That's all we ate. From then on we waited for someone to pick us up, but we didn't get out of there until the evening.

"Then at around 7:00 or 8:00 p.m. people started coming for us, but each of them picked up only a few of us. I ended up riding in a car, in a van, one of those that have tarps on the back. All of us who would fit got in there, we were covered with the tarp and we took off. We were taken to the ranch of a person who was in contact with the man who brought us. Once we got there we had dinner and they let us bathe there. We slept in that house and the next day we left. Finally the car left me in Santa Ana, California. Only a few of us got to California, many others were going to Chicago. Different cars would pick them up.

"I came with two girls - two men brought us in a car. We arrived in Santa Ana and they wanted to drop me off in Los Angeles. But, Tomás, who was in communication with the coyotes, said, 'No.' He asked them to bring me up to the Bay Area. The man said that they could not bring me up here and said he was going to leave me there in Santa Ana, but he said that if my husband wanted to, he could send me by plane to San Jose, California. When the coyote spoke to Tomás, he told him to send them money to buy me a ticket for the plane. That was on top of the $1,200. They bought me a change of clothes just because I was very dirty. They bought a T-shirt and trousers for me and took me to an airport and left me there. I came to San José and Tomás was waiting for me.

"When I came here I had just turned 34 years old. Tomás and I got together at that time, but nothing more. We started living together, and then we had our children. I think when our first child was four or five years old we finally got married. My husband and I are Catholic, but we were not married by a church.

"By the time I arrived in the States, Tomás had been in the U.S. for a while. He worked in a pizzeria. He worked there for 19 years. It is two years since he stopped working there, because they closed the restaurant. Now he does day work. He does yard and garden work and assists doing floors or masonry. But he does not know how to do that on his own – the company he works for tells him what to do and he does it.

"When I first got to the U.S., I started cleaning houses; but later on, when I already had children, I no longer worked. Tomás told me not to work. He said he did not know how we would look after the children if I worked. He thought that any money I'd made would be spent in day care.

I'd end up working for no money. He told me that I shouldn't work until they were old enough, until they were in school. I started attending adult school, because I said, 'I do not work and have time to study, I should go to school.' I went to adult school when my younger son started going to kindergarten and my older one was in elementary school. I learned a lot, because when I came, I knew nothing. I could count numbers only to eleven and knew no more. I didn't know the letters of the alphabet. I finished three years of adult education.

"After eleven years in the States, I wanted to work again. I had met some friends who told me that they were going to the Day Worker Center in Mt. View, California to work and that they were finding jobs. I was not working. I asked my husband, 'What if I started going to the Day Worker Center? I was told one could get a job there.' 'Well, go there if you want, just go.' So I started going there. Through the Center, I've worked cleaning houses and sometimes babysitting. I like everything. I have two houses I clean on a regular basis. I go once every two weeks to each. Sometimes when the owner has people over, she asks me to come every week. Since they employed us through the Center we get paid $12 an hour. But if I work for six or seven hours she gives me $120.

"If my husband works in the morning, I'll work in the afternoon. Our children go to school from 8:00 a.m. to 3:00 p.m. Tomás usually takes Pablo to school. On Wednesday morning I walk him to school. Sometimes he tells me he's going with other boys, but it's not common. He always asks me to walk him and he calls me to tell me if is he is coming back or to see if his dad did not go to work so that he'll pick him up. Leandro walks or rides his skateboard or bicycle.

"My older son, Leandro, likes skateboarding. The younger liked the scooter. One Sunday the family went to a park and on that day my son said, 'Can I bring the scooter?' 'Take it.' We went through the park and down a bridge. As we were descending, the older boy had already been there, and on that day the younger one was wearing flip-flops and he said, 'Lend me the scooter, I can take it' and he gave it to him. I said, 'No, no, do not go, you're going too fast and you can fall.' He grabbed the scooter anyway and was going really fast and fell when he was going down the hill. I was afraid he'd fall on one side and continue rolling down. He fell and he could not stop; he wanted to stop with his foot, lower it to break, and I think the flip-flop made him fall. He scraped his arm, knee, face, and forehead. He was crying and no longer wanted to use the scooter.

"The younger son, Pablo, is now 13, and the older, Leandro is turning 15. He's a year and a half older. We speak only Spanish to our children. They started to learn English when they started to go to school. The younger boy started going to preschool and learning his first few English words. He would sing in English. Then in kindergarten, they learned more English. Pablo is a good student, but the older boy finds it harder. Leandro says he does not like school. He keeps asking, 'Why was school invented?' I tell him, 'How do you ask that! If there were no school ... ' He is attending high school now. He says he does not like it, he thinks it's boring. I tell him he must study so that when he is older he can be whatever he wants. He says he wants to be a football player. He likes to play and wants to be a professional football player. I tell him, 'To be that you also have to keep studying.'

"On weekends, sometimes, we go to the movies. I do not like the movies very much, but the older boy does. Because he likes those movies and I do not like them, I fall asleep in the cinema. I do not like the films that he likes best, so I ask his dad to take him. Even if he doesn't like them, he takes him. My son will tell you over and over that he wants to go. The younger one doesn't. Sometimes he says he will go too but then says: 'No, I'll go another day to see a movie that I really like.'

"I want them to be smart kids and really become something, for them to have good families and get along. I want them to have wives and children and also be a good parent, for them to live well when they build their families. They used to fight a lot before and right now Leandro plays tricks on his younger brother, but they play. As soon as they start playing I know how it will end. So I say, 'Please peace, peace please!' And then comes the younger one and says, 'Leandro did this to me!' 'You wanted to play with him too,' I say.

"Well, I think I am a good mother to my children and they listen to the advice I give them. Although they sometimes do not want to hear it or they don't understand it yet, in the end I'd like them to think that it was good advice I was giving them. They are good kids and I am proud to have them be my children. They are already so big, they are growing and I say that when they're little, one says 'Oh! And I want them to grow!' and now when they are older, 'Oh! I wish they were babies!' And then I see pictures of when they were young children and say, 'Oh! Look at how beautiful they are!'

"Right now, we live in an apartment in Sunnyvale, CA. It is a two-bedroom apartment, and like every other apartment it has its living room, kitchen, bathroom; it has a balcony. The boys share a room. We rent it for $1,650 each month. Our biggest expenses are rent, food and bills.

"To help make the rent, we rented our sofa in our living room, to a person that we trusted. That person said that we were like family to him and we also thought of him as family. He was a 32 year-old man. We met him because he lived with some friends of ours, and he said he wanted to move out of there because it was too expensive and he had to share the room. There were about five people in the room and he did not want to stay there because they charged a lot.

"We already had someone sleeping on our sofa, but when that person vacated, the man asked my husband again, and Tomás told him we were moving. We had already been asked to move because the apartment was going to get remodeled. They asked us all to leave. My husband said, 'If you want to come you can, but in a few days we're leaving.' 'Yes, I'm going there' and he came to live in our house. We spent fifteen days in the old apartment and then we moved and he continued living with us for about two years.

"One day, this past year, Pablo realized that his brother had left his Facebook account open, on the computer. He told me about the account being open. He said, 'Leandro said he doesn't have a girlfriend, but he has a photo with this girl.' I asked, 'How do you know?' 'He left his Facebook page open.' 'Did you close it?' 'No.' I wanted to see and I started to look at his Facebook page - but it already seemed to me like something was off. When we looked at the computer we understood that the man renting our sofa was abusing him. He lived in our house! It was the hardest thing for our family.

"The day I realized what was happening, because my younger son showed me, Leandro was not home. We had given him permission to stay overnight at the home of one of his friends. Before he went, I talked to his friend's mom - the boy's mother. My son did not know we knew anything at the time and, as the man was single, we did not tell him anything when we realized the situation.

"I used to leave Leandro with that person and take the younger one with me, on Saturdays when I had to go downtown or anywhere. When they didn't have to go to school, I'd take Pablo with me. I thought then that the guy is a male and the child was a boy, too. I thought nothing could go wrong in that case.

"And then a day came when I had a bad feeling about it. I do not know why, but I already sensed something, because I thought, 'Oh! I hope he's not teaching him bad things.' I started wondering what they might be doing. As the day came, the day when I realized, something came to my mind. I thought that he may have messages or conversations with this person and I started to look for that on Facebook and there were a lot where he would threaten the boy. My husband and I were so shocked and so ashamed for our family.

"When I saw everything, I took the computer away because I was in my son's room, and I did not want Pablo to see. I went to the kitchen and my younger son asked, 'Why are you going out there?' 'I'm tired of sitting here in bed. I'll go there to the table in the kitchen.' I went and there I began to see everything. Then I told my husband 'Come, come, I want you to see this!' 'What is it?' 'I think, this is wrong' 'But what?' 'I want you to see it yourself, sit down and see this.' I felt like I was filled with rage, I do not know, I felt my body, inside, I was shaking. We did not know what to do! 'What should we do? This is not right, this is wrong.'

"At that time the man was not home so my husband told me, 'I'll talk to him when he gets home.' 'You know what, if you talk to him, do you know what he will do? He is going to go away and what if he remains in contact with Leandro?' 'Yes, how should we do it, then? Should we talk with the two of them together?' And I said, 'What will happen then is that he is going to go away from here; I do not want him to be here.' We found ourselves not knowing what to do, because if we kicked him out he would go but he could still be in contact with Leandro or he could do something to him.

"Two days passed and then the boys were on vacation from school one week and then on that day, Monday, it was a holiday, and everything was closed. We told the child's godparents what was happening and they suggested we go to a community-counseling center and ask to see someone who could help us there. When we arrived, we were told it was only by appointment. But when they saw us, when we told them what we were going through, that it was urgent and we wanted advice, they saw us. We showed them the computer, where we had the proof of everything.

"When we showed the counselor, she said she had to call another office, Child Protective Services. They said that what was happening was a crime, what that person was doing was a crime. The man was of age and that Leandro was just a child. Then we talked to this other person, who asked, 'Are you willing to let the police intervene?' We said, 'Yes. We must do that.' They said they were going to call them and let us talk to them. We talked there and told them what was happening and the police said, 'Go home. In a few minutes a person will come by your house and talk to you.' and we were told to stay in the house, a person would come.

"When Leandro wanted to leave the house, we told him, 'You're not going to go anywhere.' 'Why?' 'Because a teacher will come to talk to you.' 'What did I do?' 'I do not know. We want to know, too.' In reality, we did not want to tell him anything.

"Later that evening the police arrived, one detective and a social worker. The detective and the social worker spoke Spanish. They talked with Leandro who said nothing, because the man had threatened him and told him, 'You can't say anything, anything.' Then the detective took my son to the police department, because he would not talk very much at home. The detective said she was going to take him, so that they could talk privately, so that my son could talk more freely, if we gave them permission, and if we wanted to, we could also go.

"We all went to the police department. We waited for my son and finally, the man was detained. He is still in jail. Leandro is better, but what I am afraid of is that when the man is freed, I don't know what is going to happen. We do not know how many years he'll be given, because the case is still not closed, because the man has not declared himself guilty. He does not have papers here. He is still in prison, and we don't know what will happen. We are still scared.

"I have been in the United States for 15 years. My children were both born here and are citizens. Right now, I have no papers to go to Mexico, so I have to stay. I would like for something to get done so that we would have papers to be here, that we could at least get a work permit. My children can apply for green cards for us, but they cannot do that until they are 21 years old. By that time, I think we'll be old.

"Our challenge is to learn to speak English, because in many places where there is work they want you to know English. I communicate, but not very well. It depends on the type of work and what you need to do. They usually ask for us to be able to communicate with the employer well. Of course our children speak English well. And if we mispronounce things, they laugh. They say, 'You do not know, do not know,' and that is why we are learning. Anything we don't know we then ask them, 'How would you say this?' and then they tell us.

"If I had papers I'd like to go back home to visit, but I would return. I want to live here. I would be here and there, on both sides. Because I don't think my children want to go and I'd rather stay here with my children. My children are the most important thing, my family and work. Work to keep on getting by, at least. If someday, something happens to me and I get sent back to Mexico, I will not be able to get back to the U.S. It is harder to pass through the border now.

"In a few years I think that I will no longer be able to work. 'What shall we do?' I think about what will happen when we're old folks and if we are still here in the States. I do not know if my children will want us to be living with them. I think if they do not want us to be living with them, then it would be better if we were in Mexico. But life is better here."

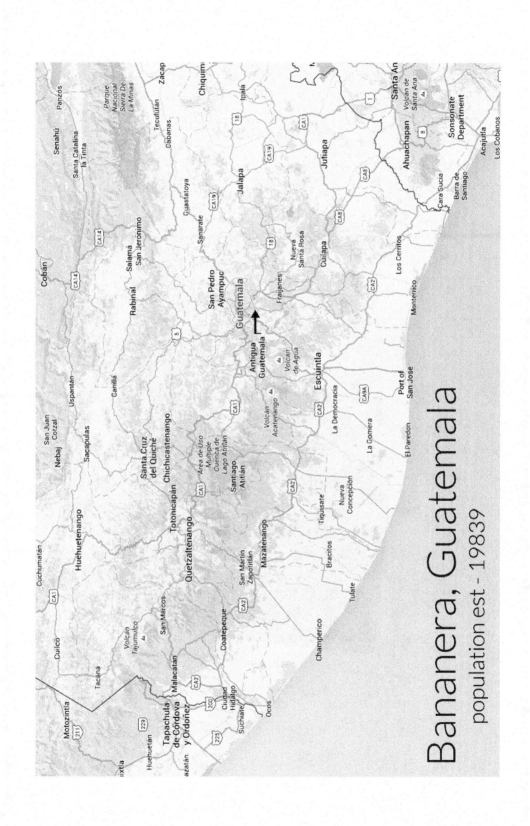

Bananera, Guatemala
population est - 19839

Chapter 4

Ruben's Story

"I am not unhappy, but I am not happy. I'm from Guatemala City, the capital of Guatemala. When I came to the U.S. in 2002, the rest of my family was already in the States and they were all American citizens. I had a wife and two small children, who were living with me in Guatemala. My mom, who was also living in Guatemala, got sick. My siblings in America wanted my mom to come and spend Christmas in the U.S. But my mom did not want to go if my children, her grandchildren, and my wife didn't come with her.

"We were doing well in Guatemala. I always had good jobs. I worked with my head, nothing physical. But, to please my mom, I requested three visas, one for my wife and two for my children. After a while I received them. Then I presented my passport. I had been coming to the U.S. since the 1980's on work related trips. I never liked the U.S. as a place to live. But that time, as I said, my mom would only travel if my wife and my children traveled with her. Since everyone had their visa, I only had to give them the money to fly over and spend Christmas and New Years in the States. I did not travel with them because I was working as an industry supervisor. After three months in the U.S., my family did not want my mom, or my children, or my wife to return to Guatemala. They wanted me to travel to the States. That's why I'm here. I do not regret the decision for them, I regret it for me.

"So when I entered the U.S. I had a visa. The owner of the company I worked for in Guatemala cleared me because I had I traveled with him to the U.S. and other Central American countries to buy spare parts for machinery. I knew a little English, because it was necessary to know a little English to buy machinery.

"I stayed - overstayed. I don't have a green card. My brother started the paperwork for me to be legal. I had to pay $700 to start the process. The papers are still being processed - they entered them in 2001, and right now, one month before 2001 is being processed (2000). It's a matter of time, nothing else. I talked to the lawyer and he explained, I can fix those papers, but you would have to leave the U.S. and live in Guatemala for 10 years. The lawyer advised me, 'No, do not go, you better wait here because laws change here. Sooner or later the law will be changed here and you'll be able to arrange your papers here. There'll be no need for you to leave.' I asked what advantages or disadvantages I'd have if there were reforms, and he told me that I could only get advantages, because all my information has been submitted, and there is no need to look for anything else.

"I was born in Guatemala, in a place called Bananera on January 9, 1953. My dad told me he went for a walk with me, and did not know what to name me. 'The first friend to greet me, that's what I will name him.' He met a man who was big, and called Ruben Pena. 'I'm going to name him Ruben,' and so he did. I only have one name.

"I take after my dad. He was of Spanish descent, but was born in Guatemala. My mom was from Mazatenango, Guatemala. They met at a baseball game and they stayed together. They lived nearly 65 years together and got married after about 40 years of being together, after having built their family. We were already grown when they got married.

"We are 5 siblings - three females and two males. Now the oldest is 69. She's called Argentina. Followed by Leticia, who is 66. Then Graciela, she is 64. Then me at 61, and Robert, 56 years old. All five alive and kicking. My sister Argentina lives in Palo Alto, CA. The other sister, Leticia, is staying with them, because she is on vacation here. She lives in Guatemala. My brother also lives here in Palo Alto, CA. The three live together in an apartment. I also live in Palo Alto, but not with them.

"My dad worked to provide for us all. He was fine carpenter of furniture. He worked for a company and also did rustic pieces, but his specialty was fine carpentry. I remember my dad a lot - for me he was not only my father, he was also my friend. My mother as well, but with my dad a little more, because he was a man. One relates more. We played ball, etc. I waited for him as 'water in May ' (an expression in Guatemala, the rains that everyone is waiting for to plant), so I waited for my father to play ball.

"I spent my childhood in Bananera, until I was 25 years old. It gets confusing for me: Bananera, Guatemala City, the U.S. ... all of it together. In Guatemala we begin working when we are very young. As my father was my friend, I went to work with him. 'I'll help you,' he said, and he gave me a few pennies, and I was happy. Seeing my father work too much was difficult for me. In our town, at the age of 18 years, one could legally work. I had to talk to the mayor and ask him to add a year to my age. I wanted to begin working to help my dad. In those places it is hard to live. I said, 'I do not want to live like my father lived.'

"When my dad was working, when I was young, we lived in a small wooden house. As I grew older, I told my dad that I wanted to make a house where he and my mom could have a room with a bathroom inside, where I could have a room with a bathroom inside, and about three more rooms for when my family comes to visit from U.S., for them to live here. I started designing it on paper. It was going to be a comfortable house. I laid everything out. I was the architect of this house. I had seen a house I liked, and I made some scribbles and then I drew it the same as the one I liked. I gave the drawing to the mason, and he made it.

"Our home was in a very good neighborhood. Where we lived, if you did not have sugar that afternoon to sweeten your coffee you could go to anyone in the neighborhood and say, 'Could you lend me a cup of sugar?' And they would lend it to you, and you would return the favor some other time. Over here, in the U.S., you can lend but it won't be returned.

"In primary school, I liked going to school in the morning. I returned home at noon and we had to do our homework; we couldn't play until we finished. When we finished our homework we had lunch, and ran out to play ball. We helped my mother to do the housework, because we each had our tasks. It's your turn to bring water, your turn to sweep, your turn do the dishes ... we all had our chores. But everyone had a good time doing our tasks. There were no fights over it - it was all in order. I wash the dishes, you sweep, we didn't leave everything for my mom to do, because as I said, we were 5 children, and leaving everything for my mom to do was too heavy for her.

"Everyone else said, 'I will go to the U.S. to help my children make it.' But my dad did not think that, my dad said, 'I will help my children here.' He had another mindset, but a good one. And he helped us get through. When we got older, his first child moved, and then another and in the end three went to the States and two stayed in Guatemala. I did not leave my dad and my mom. I got married and had my dad and my mom with me. My father died; he is buried in Guatemala. My mother became ill, and came here (to the States). And then I came. My mother died in 2003, she is buried here in a cemetery in the U.S. That is the problem and that is one of the reasons why I'm still here. And what's done is done and one cannot take it back.

"The most important thing for my parents was to help their children be successful. I completed primary, secondary and some years in a school for a teaching career. It did not seem long. The company my father worked for provided education and health insurance for primary school. It was one of the best schools in Guatemala. It was called Dolores Bedoya de

Molina and my father's company paid for it. After that, I went to a private school, where he had to pay for our education.

"I liked mathematics. I learned from my dad. I did well, and was a good student in mathematics. I read a story of Socrates, where he had to add a list of numbers. First he added pairs and then the odd numbers he left behind. When he finished adding the even he would just grab the odd points. In Guatemala when you bought something, the shopkeepers wrote it down in their little booklets. When the shop owner grabbed the calculator, my dad would tell him, 'You know, tell me the numbers and I'll do the math.' 'Okay'. The owner would tell him 2.13, 5.22, 4… And my dad said, 'It is this much.' And the other man would begin adding with the calculator, 10 minutes later … he got the same number… And that is how I learned from my dad how to operate with numbers. I have worked in establishments and companies in purchasing and sales and was scolded by a supervisor because of how I add to and fro looking for pairs, leaving the odds. And when I finished with the pairs I see a 5 and another 5 and another 5, I say 15 once, I don't say 5 plus 5 plus 5 … if there is four 5's I just add an even 20. He did not care, and the supervisor scolded me and said, 'That is not how you add.' And I said, 'While the result remains the same, you can add however you want.' And that is good.

"I started attending the teaching college, although I did not get to the end of it. That's when we moved to Guatemala City. I studied for 11 years of elementary school, 3 of high school and 3 more of teacher's school. 17 years in total. I was still young and if I had a little more schooling it would have been better.

"I would have liked to be an asphalt engineer, because I realized that many numbers and calculations are used in that field. In meters, logs … everything is achieved through numbers. And, as I said, I have always liked numbers. But it didn't happen. At that time, pursuing that type of career was very expensive. And I started to work and I liked the money. When I started, my first job was to sweep. You swept for a while and then were moved to a better spot. I swept the whole factory for three months. Then the most sophisticated machine in the factory caught my attention. During my lunch hour, my free time, I would help the other workers, and the owners noticed and moved me to the largest machine. What I learned in the first factory where I worked sweeping, I put to good use. After a while, another company called me and asked me to help make their factory work.

"I worked in Guatemala in the companies Corrugadora Guatemala, Cartones de Guatemala, Empaques San Lucas, Cajas y Empaques de El Salvador, and Empaques de Costa Rica. Everything about cardboard. When I focus my attention on one thing, I like to solve it. It is certain that there are engineers who are engineers, perhaps, because they buy their diploma. I am not an engineer, but I was better than the engineers. Because I already came with my ideas, and said, 'This is not true, so let's do this better.' They would say, 'I studied for this.' 'Well, I did not, but I have many years of work in this industry and I know it like the palm of my hand, so let's do it this way, it is better.' And it was.

"In the last factory I worked in, we were in a village or town, and we went to lunch by plane - from that village to the city, 20 minutes, just to go to lunch. We were the owner, supervisors, and me. Six of us went to lunch. When we returned, everyone who worked for me, fifteen men, told me, 'Why don't you eat with us?' They ate there in a humble little dining room. I spoke with the boss and said, 'I'm not going to go to lunch with you; I'll go to lunch with my workers. The boss said, 'Well then go, all we can do is pay for your lunch.'

"My wife only completed elementary school, when we were coming to the States. I had requested visas for them. The first thing the embassy asked for was for a letter of recommendation and we asked an evangelical pastor and the evangelical pastor denied us. He told us that they could not lie. I said, 'Then say she works for you, that she is your secretary.' 'I cannot lie,' he said. 'Well, thank you very much.' I went to another priest and explained my problem and asked, 'Can you help me?' 'Sure,' he said. Because the other priest denied me; I could not lie to the second priest. He said, 'If I knew that what I do is for you to use it in something bad, that is one thing, but you are not going to do anything wrong, you will use it for something good.' He did it. The problem was when he came to the embassy with us, they asked my wife, 'You are the secretary?' 'Yes.' 'Here you have a computer, press the L.' My wife put all her fingers together and pressed every key. The consul was a good person because he realized why she did that and approved the visa. At least I can use the computer; I got my first diploma typing. I did it years ago. I have not forgotten where the letters are.

"So I did not come to the U.S. to make money. Money was never a problem. I didn't have too much, but I always had money. I never used a checkbook or credit card in Guatemala; I used cash. I liked to carry no less than 15 thousand quetzales in my wallet, whenever I was traveling. It was my decision was that my mother, my wife and my two children should come to the States. And they never returned. I joined them, but the reality is, that I am not very happy to be in the U.S. I wish I had stayed in Guatemala. I haven't lost hope of returning. The owners of the factories over there are still calling me. When they call me they say, 'Where are you working?' and I lie, I tell them I'm in a factory that I used to work at. I'm not going to say I'm gardening, or cutting trees, that's my business.

"When I came to U.S. I went to my sister's home - my mother, my wife and my two children were there. They all are American citizens. Only my wife, my children and I are not. I started working in construction on a building in San Francisco. My nephew got me the job. My nephew worked there and asked me if I wanted to work with him and I said, 'Yes,' because I was out of work. He would drive me there and back. But those are temporary jobs, the house was completed and the work stopped.

"When that job finished, I started caring for a gentleman here in Palo Alto. He was a millionaire. I worked with him and he paid very well. I earned around $10,000 a month. I took care of him from 4:00 p.m. until 10:00 a.m. the next day, Monday through Friday. On Saturday I started working at 4:00 in the afternoon and left on Monday. So, I spent all night Saturday and all day Sunday until Monday morning at his home and then left again. He would even say, 'This weekend come with your wife and two children,' as he had enough room. He was alone; his whole family lived in New York. I had a good time with him. Unfortunately, he was too sick and I only worked with him for eight months before he died. He used to give us his credit card to pay for everything in the house. Of course, we had to send the receipts to his children so they could see how everything was being handled.

"He died, and his children were very good people, and gave me a good settlement. When I finished that, I lost my job, and as I had some money I said, 'Well, let's take a break.' But the money runs out, and I started to look for work, I kept searching and searching... until they told me about the Day Worker Center. That is how I got here and I have been here ever since.

"At the Day Worker Center they have a variety of jobs for us. They ask us to work and we don't even know what kind of work we are going to do. It's not like when you have your work, for example, as a chef. Every day you know that you are going to cook. Not at the Center. Here it is 'I need two workers for one thing,' and the next day it will be for something else. When they come to tell me that there is work, I ask, 'What is it?' If it is electrical work, I better leave it for someone else. I'd like a system here in the Center where businesses can come to give us more work, because here we sometimes spend whole days doing nothing.

"Sometimes I get jobs I don't even know how to start. All I know is that I will finish it, and before I know it, when I look up, I didn't know where to start and I am already finished. Once a man who lived nearby hired me, and told me, before you start I want you to watch these videos on the computer. And we sat at the computer and began to see the videos. He wanted me to plant some grass, but artificial grass. And I asked, 'Where am I going to do that?' 'There.' But the place where he wanted to do it was a dump. I had to clean it up, remove branches, garbage, clean it; it took me almost eight days to do everything. After I finished, it turned out really nice and I said, 'What a change!' He took a photo before and an after picture when the work was finished. There was a difference, quite a difference.

"I like gardening and moving mostly. In summer there is a lot of yard work, but in winter it stops. An hour ago I was called for a job. If I had time, they would send me to do some gardening. But as I had this commitment for this interview, I told them no, I couldn't right now. Send someone else or I can go after the end of the interview or maybe tomorrow, since we had agreed on this a while ago. I did not want to miss it.

"I get up at about 5:00 a.m., I shower; I do not like staying in bed. It is not for me. They say that when one is already an adult, resting is just a way to wait for death. My dad, at three or four was already up. He did not sleep or let my mom sleep, because he would go to the kitchen and start making coffee. And it is true, we all go through that, eventually. At 7:00 a.m. I am already ready to come to the Center. I have had breakfast. I even watch the news. I see many people at the Center who drink their coffee here because they had no time at home. There is always time, it's just that they don't make the time, because there is time for everything.

"If I don't go to work, I am at the Day Worker Center until 2:00 in the afternoon. For those who do not work, life here is hard. If I do not work I have to try and figure something else out. And, it gives me no pain or shame to admit it, I go to the parks to find cans, bottles, recycling. I save. I will wash cars. I hope that someone recommends me to another person. Three days a week, I teach a few ladies English. They are studying English at the park. There is a public school where they teach English, but the English they teach is a bit advanced. So these women do not understand much, and they have asked me to help them, and they pay me. I earn my pennies here and there. I earn my cents. I'm not lazy.

"Full time work is very difficult to get right now without papers. Especially at this time. A year ago, I got a job as a dishwasher. I had already worked as a dishwasher in another restaurant, but they had closed because the owner sold the place and when the new owner arrived, he fired us all. So I got the job as a dishwasher in another restaurant and they didn't even have to teach me, I already had the experience. What a great experience! Right? Putting dishes in the machine and removing them. Well, I did the cleaning and then I had time to take a break. The owner told me, 'Look Ruben, I think you should come to work every other day.' I said, 'But why? Every other day? One day in and a day out?' 'Because I see that you have enough time to rest. Better that the day you do not come to work all those dishes will accumulate for the next day and you will have enough work to do.' I told him 'I'm sorry, but you want me to work a two-day job in one day? I rest because I work fast. If you do not want me to rest, I will work slower.' 'No, I'd rather you only came every other day.' 'No, you know what? Pay me for the days I have worked and thank you very much.'

"The truth is that here in the Day Worker Center, one is lucky. If you work with Americans, you can establish a little life here at the Center. Sometimes you get to work for different kinds of people. There are Americans, Hindus and Chinese. The truth is, I do not know if it's good to say, but there are people who are not good. For me, the best people to work for are Americans. They realize the work you do, which is very easy but they cannot do it and they take it into account. But there are other people watching you work and saying, 'I could have done that myself.' I say, 'But then why didn't you? I wouldn't have needed to come here.' There are all kinds of people. Last week I could only work for two days, but one American lady was good and she paid us as if we had worked all week.

"I do not have friends, real friends, at the Day Worker Center. I have acquaintances. I wanted to find a friend here in the United States, but have not found one yet. I've realized that a person, who has enough, does not want me to have as much as him. Even among us, there is selfishness.

"If I do not have work, I come home, unless my wife wants me to run errands. Then I go to the park to see what I can find. I wait until night to see if I'm going to teach the ladies I told you about. And, literally, that is it. Last night they brought me to a child to babysit. Another night I cared for another lady's child. I get paid $25 a night just for the child to fall asleep there. I'm watching him, sleeping next to him. At six in the morning they pick him up. Here you have to do everything you can to earn money. You have to do everything.

"I met my wife, Romelia Arevalo in Guatemala. When I built the large house I designed, her family rented our small house next door. It was love at first sight or love at last sight, but well, that was how I met her. As our houses were next to each other, when I returned home from work, I do not know if by chance or if she knew my time to arrive, she came to the door of the house where they lived and I greeted her. It was every day and I said, 'This is not a coincidence,' and already my heart had begun to beat a little faster and that's how we began a relationship that has continued to where we are now.

"Because of the jobs I've had, there were women who wanted to be with me. Because I was an important person in business, I drove around in my own car and when I worked for the company they would put me in a company car, with my driver. And women then realized, 'If I stay with him I'll be fine.' But at that time I did not think of finding a woman for me. I dated them, but not to formalize a life. Until my wife was the one who got me. And here I am, 22 years later, still with her. And sometimes I ask her, 'Aren't you bored of me by now?' 'No,' she says.

"The truth is that I have been with my wife 22 years, but we were not married for many years. As I told you before, my brother who lives in the U.S. filed the paperwork for us to stay here. I had to marry her in order to be eligible to stay. We got married in 1999.

"My wife taught me many things. Before I met her, I did not have any meaning in my life. If I wanted to, I would come home early or come home late, or not come home. Now I try my best to get home at 2:00 in the afternoon. Many at the Center say, 'Why would I want to go home? If I am at my house I'm alone. The apartment owner does not want us to be there during the day because we make noise.' I agree with them. They are right. They have no one to take a piece of bread to. They are alone. If I were alone I would also spend my time on the street, but I'm not alone. I have someone to see. Even though, as in every home, there are a few discussions. It is healthy to argue a bit.

"As I mentioned, I have two children. The female, Wendy, is the oldest; she was born on May 12, 1994, the boy, Julio Ruben was born on April 12, 1996. They have gotten so big already. Right now my son is working selling donuts. My daughter's husband will not let her work. He works at a car dealership.

"The pride that I have right now is that my daughter got married and made me a grandfather. And my son, that is 18, has not gotten married, yet, but he is living with a girl, and also gave me a grandson. Two grandchildren one month apart. My grandchildren are both boys. My daughter's son is Abraham and my son's is named Antonio. Right now the most important thing for me, as a proud old man, are my grandchildren. Always in good times and in bad, we are there for each other. Especially now with these two grandchildren, I'm more united than I am alone.

"Five of us live together - my wife, my son, his girlfriend, my grandson and me. We live in an apartment in Palo Alto. My daughter lives with her husband in Sunnyvale. The apartment where we live charges us $1,200 per month in rent. It has a bedroom, a living room, a kitchen and bathroom. The cheapest thing you can have. And they are charging that because we have been renting there for quite a while. I take care of the rent. My son is responsible for food and bills, along with my wife, because she works, too. She works at The Donut Shop. My son also works at The Donut Shop. My wife worked there, and a boy resigned, and my son was looking for work and my wife had several years working there. She spoke to the boss and the boss hired our son. They get paid in cash.

"My main problem right now is economics. What I care about is income. Sometimes there is not enough income, and my son and wife help me with the rent. I think not only me, but also all the people at the Center have trouble paying the rent. Well, I'm beating it, because, as I say, I'm here, I'm there, I'm here, there. If I sit waiting to see if money will fall from the sky, it won't. That's the hardest part. In the U.S. you can find food anywhere. Clothes, you find anywhere. Where to live is the most difficult. If I have enough for the rent, I do not worry. Half the time I do not have enough, and I have to find a way.

"When I am not working, I like to read, mostly the Bible. I like to read and watch television. At least from what I understood when I was watching the History Channel, there are forty generations before ours. All these unknowns are things I like. I like to learn. I like to cook; I do not know if you know that meat we call *ranchera*. They are a few slices of steak and I like to throw them on the grill with all their concoctions, flavors, to release the scent. Some onions, rice, and some chili. I usually do it on Sundays.

"Sometimes we go to parties. I drink a couple of beers, but I like to be careful who I do that with, because sometimes there are people who may have something bottled up inside. When there are some beers involved it comes to light. And, for me, I never liked it.

"I also do things with my wife. Sometimes I say, 'We got old!' 'Let's go out, just the two of us. Let's see if we remember anything from when we were young!' And we leave together and go to a restaurant to eat. Because all the rest of the time we are taking care of everyone else. We get along well. Of course in the Bible it says, 'Therefore, a man leaves his father and mother' and the woman also says the same thing 'and will join her husband and they will become one person.'

"I believe that there is one God. I trust, really trust, in God. I also depend on him and on myself because I'm not hopeful to be sustained by someone else. On Sunday, I go to a Protestant church. Not to kill time but to listen to the minister, and I listen to the good advice he gives, because even though the minister is human and he might not say all good things, I take the good and discard the bad. Protestant gospel. Most people in Guatemala are Catholic. My parents were Catholic. The truth is that I changed because of where I want to get to in life. After a Catholic baptism, there is a party, beer and liquor. They start to fight - men with men, women with women. That does not happen in the religion in which I am now. There are baptisms, too; they dip the baby in the water, and we all eat quietly, no beer, no liquor, no nothing. That was my reason why I changed. I even have a friend who sent for her dad to Guatemala to celebrate a Catholic baptism. Her father came to the States and to this date he is in prison, because at the party he had an argument with my friend, and killed him and he is in jail.

"I have faced my life and solved problems. I do not know how I did it, but I think I've solved them well. In my future I would like to improve, I'd like it to improve from what I'm going through right now. When I am gone, I would like to be remembered for the good things, not bad things. For even though one has been bad, you know very well that a dead man is never bad. From the moment he dies people say, 'Poor thing, he was so good!' - even if he was the worst person.

"I intend to return to Guatemala and my dad at some point. My family does not want to, but I can't adapt here. You might live next to someone and not even know them. Not there. In Guatemala, the neighborhood is your family. Something happens to you in the morning, knock on the neighbor's door and the neighbor will help you. Here, if something happens at dawn, you knock on your neighbor's door ... he is either asleep or he will not open the door, and the next day you go and talk to them and they tell you, 'You should have knocked harder.' The truth is, I've noticed that people are selfish - mostly those that are doing well. They do not want those who are doing worse to catch up with them. In other places where I've been, it's never like that.

"The problem is that my only family still living in Guatemala, is my sister. Everyone else is here. And as we have always been united, we want everyone to be here. My family tells me to be patient. With papers I can go back to Guatemala and then I can return to the U.S. My wife likes it here. She is happy here, because she has her two children, two grandchildren, and her little job. I say, 'I know that you are well here, because you were never okay there in Guatemala.' But if I went back to Guatemala, I could work for one of the same companies as before.

"Maybe I am too old for change and improvement. Not only here, even in Guatemala they're telling me that no one will give you a job once you are over 30. As I say, both in Guatemala and here in America, if you have friends, you get a job, but without friends you cannot get work. I have a nephew here, an American citizen, good English, and he spent years without working, sending letters here, sending letters, applications, and nothing. Until at last he spoke to his sister-in-law and through her he got a job. Now he is the manager of a hotel. But, he is a citizen, he has good English, and it was still hard. Let alone one being illegal, it's even harder.

"One thinks about it, but as we say, the future is not known. To God one day is as a thousand years and a thousand years is one day. I would like to be a nice old man, a kind old man. I do not want to ever be prostrated. The culture we have in the U.S., which our children have been learning, is that when one gets old they want to put you into an asylum. I would not like that, because in our culture, the grandparents come first, his coffee cup, his sweet bread, everything for him first. Not here. Here grandpa is a burden.

"To regret, regret, what's done is done. I regret having come to the United States. Well, life has taught me many things, both good and bad. I tried to ignore the bad and keep the good. But sometimes, as the apostle Paul says, 'Why do I do what I should not do and what I should, I do not do.' Every mind is a world on its own, we are human, and we make mistakes."

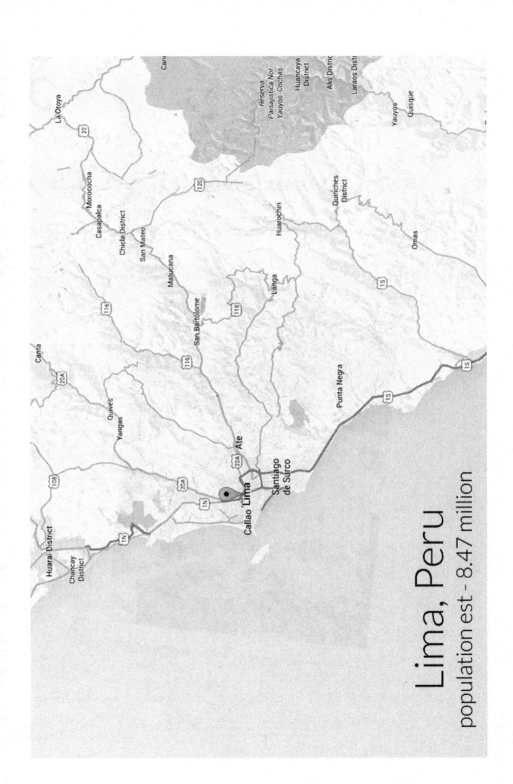

Lima, Peru

population est - 8.47 million

Chapter 5

Aurora's Story

"In 1999, my son Andrés, who lives in the United States, sent me a letter of invitation, asking me to come visit him in the Bay Area. He is really not my son, he is my nephew, but I raised him since his childhood. I am like a mother to him. He calls me mom because I raised him since he was a small boy. My sister died and his father was already dead, so I kept my nephew and raised him as my own child. Since I was single at the time, I was the only one who could take him. My other sisters were married and living away from home outside of Lima, Peru.

"My nephew was in the Peruvian military when he came to the States. At that time, the situation in the country, with the rebel group Shining Path was very difficult. Andrés sought and obtained political asylum and has his papers. He lives in a rented house in Los Altos, California and works for NASA, doing maintenance. He married and had two daughters. When they were young girls, Andrés brought his daughters to me in Lima. He took them to me because, according to him, the education was better in Peru.

"When Andrés invited me to the States, I was able to obtain a tourist visa for 6 months and flew from Lima to Dallas, for a stopover, and then to San Francisco. I brought my nephew's daughters back with me to the States. I brought them back to their parents when the oldest was 15 years old.

"My life in Lima was okay – I could not complain. I had a steady job and earned a little money. I could just support myself. When my nephew Andrés sent me the ticket to the U.S., my desire wasn't to stay here. I asked my employer for six months' leave without pay and vacation. I wanted to go back to Peru, because I had work there.

"After I arrived, I did not want to be here doing nothing for 6 months. Everyone in the family went out – to work or school - and I was alone in the house. So I thought, to entertain myself, I'll go to work and will work until I leave. I turned in job applications and was called and started working almost immediately. I thought I could use the money to pay for my ticket back or other expenses.

"I worked for a lady, taking care of her five year old child. The woman was a teacher, so I began work at 7:00 a.m., and came home at 3:00 pm. I also got a job at a movie theater at the Shoreline Theaters in Mt. View, California. At that time, they were not so concerned about immigration papers or work visas. I worked from 4:00 p.m. until closing at 2:00 a.m.

or whenever the last showing ended. The last film sometimes started at 12:00 a.m., and because we still made popcorn or coffee or whatever, we had to stay until it was over. We had to leave everything clean when we closed.

"I slept little, because I had to get up at 6:00 and go to work. I was used to it because in my country I worked in a hospital and sometimes I had the shift from 7:00 a.m. to 7:00 p.m. and sometimes 7:00 p.m. to 7:00 a.m.

"At Shoreline Theater, I worked the cash register and worked in the cafeteria. I would refill the condiments for the snack bar. So I had to open large cans of ketchup, mustard and jalapeños and put the contents in smaller containers. I worked for them for several months and was going to let them know I was leaving my job, since I was going to return to Lima the next day. I already had my return ticket.

"But I had an accident! I cut my hand, tendon and nerve. I had always opened the cans before with no problem. But that day, when the can I was holding was tough to open, I pressed hard, and the can, one of those large, round ones, slipped and deeply cut my left wrist. I was bleeding a lot and the company called emergency. They took me to the hospital and they stitched my wounds superficially.

"I even called to postpone my ticket... I thought that in eight days they'd take the stitches out and I would be fine. But no, when they took the stitches out, I had lost all mobility in my hand. I couldn't move it, not even my arm. My tendon and nerve had been cut through.

"So I did not plan to stay. My story was not to be here, because I had my work in Lima. Even though I earned very little, it was a steady job. But I stayed because I had to have surgery again. The company and I saw a lawyer and I told the lawyer what had happened to me. I told her I had to travel and she said, 'Do not travel! You'll stay handicapped. You need surgery.'

"I had surgery and was in rehabilitation for 6 months. I had to work with the lawyer, but at that time, I did not know not to use a lawyer from the company. The company paid for all my medical expenses and gave me $5,250 aside as compensation. They helped me get cured and all, but I did not get much compensation. Others tell me that if I had another lawyer I would have gotten more money, because, even today, this hand does not work for me. This happened when I was 54 years old. So that is why I stayed in the U.S., in the Bay Area, after my visa expired. I am glad I stayed, but it took me away from my family and my children.

"My son Pavel lives in Arizona. After my surgery, I left my nephew's home and went to Arizona for three years. There was no work there and I had no benefits in Arizona – all the expenses were on my son. Also, I did not like the weather there – it was very hot - too hot! The sun leaves spots on your skin. I decided to return to California.

"When I arrived back from Arizona, I began living with a friend, Natividad Rosales, in a small house in Mt. View, California. I met her at the Adventist Church we both attended. We share the expenses - $900 for rent plus other expenses, like water and electricity. Rent is the main expense. First, when I work, I save for the rent. I do not spend anything. And once I have enough for it, I go to Costco and buy things there wholesale, like paper towels, toilet paper and vegetables.

"We each buy our own food and we share meals. Every time we cook we make different food. We tire of the same thing. Sometimes she cooks, sometimes I cook. We usually cook for three days and put the rest in the freezer. We are friends and go out together. We leave our house and travel. We get to know other places, go for a stroll, go out to eat.

"I had heard about the Day Worker Center from others in the neighborhood. I came and signed up. Now I do housecleaning. It is difficult to work with my hand that still does not work well. I usually work once or twice a week. It is not enough and with that alone I would starve. But I also have other work – outside the Center. I have three houses I clean on a regular basis. The pay is usually $12 per hour. Some people are good and pay $15 or even $20 per hour. But some want to pay less!

"I like cleaning homes, but the liquid cleaners are strong. I wear gloves, but I still get the smell of the products on me. Often times, people use pure Clorox and it feels as if I have an allergy. My eyes burn and cry and it's bad for the throat, too. Sometimes you get splashed. I have spotted jeans from splashes of bleach while cleaning showers.

"The Day Worker Center helps–it is a very good place to get work. It gives people who are unemployed an opportunity. I have many co-workers that I see regularly. But they are not my friends. Friends come to your house on the weekend. I only see the workers at the Center. I see faces, but sometimes I don't even know their names.

*****

"I was born in Lima, Peru in May, 1946 and I considered myself an 'orphan.' My mom, who was 42 years old, died in childbirth when I was born. My older sister raised me–she is the only mother I knew. I called my sister 'mama.' She was already married when I was born. She was the oldest, so she promised my mom she would take care of me. So I always called her mother, even after I got older and got married.

"All together we were eight siblings. There were four boys and four girls. Of course, since my mom died, I am the youngest and last female. I only have two brothers left, the others died. My brothers still live in Lima.

"My real mom was a descendant of the Japanese – her mother, my grandmother, was Japanese - but of course I did not know her. My father descended from the Spaniards. He was tall, white and thin. He worked in a cement factory, called Portla Cement, in San Juan de Miraflor. We lived in company housing. My father also bought land to build another house for himself. So I did not grow up with my dad–he was there sometimes, but he had his own house. I lived in the factory house with my mom (older sister) and her husband. It was a big house - it had 5 rooms and a store. We had a warehouse and we sold produce. My mom worked in the store. And on weekends, we helped. My dad would come and make a balance of the profits. He'd take us to buy clothes, shoes, whatever we needed, with the profit.

"My mother (older sister), her husband and my dad always told us to go out. They said, 'Go to play! But when the factory signals the day is over you must be back.' He was a very strict and very, very quiet man. He only played with me occasionally. That's what I remember of him. And then he passed away.

"It was good growing up in San Juan de Miraflores. At least it was when I was a small child. All my neighbors got together at night and played *ronda*. Sometimes I went to my neighbor's house, Mrs. Filomena, and we played 'theater'. When we played at theater, we did poetry or sang or acted. We also invented characters. We invented games and played house and cooked. We played making food. I would steal things to cook from my mom. Or I would climb to the tops of trees and bring down the fruit. We had tiny pots and had a kitchenette that we called *ronera* (rum). We put the food in the pots and pans. We had everything – the whole set.

"I attended the company school. It was a private school, because the company paid for the school. Basic, elementary education and then from there I went to high school. I went until I was 16 years old. I was not the best student, but I was more or less a good student. I loved language and history and geography.

"As I got older, I learned to knit, sew and cook. I liked it. I started with babies. I liked knitting small clothes and at school we were taught sewing. I also liked to embroider all types of bed sheets. I first made them for dolls and then I started making them for myself. I remember we had a sewing machine – a 'Singer' machine, but it was manual – you had to step on the pedal to make it move. I sewed just for me – and then for my children. Not for anyone else. I liked making little clothes for babies. Mixed clothing with bows and things like that.

"I helped my mom. She cooked during the week. Saturday and Sunday we washed clothes at our house. Her husband said so, and so we did. On Saturday, we had a half day of school and then in the afternoon, I washed clothes, then ironed them on Sunday – both my uniform and my dad's before he died.

"I had wanted to pursue a career – to enroll in military service. I had a dream to be a paratrooper, but it didn't happen. Once my father died, I had no help. I actually finished high school at night, working during the day shift. I did not study English, at all. We didn't learn it in high school; those who attended night did not get to study English. If you attended during the day, you would get the English course. Same thing with job training, sewing – all of that is suppressed during the night shift.

"After high school, I studied at a technological institute. I became a medical assistant. I worked in the hospital with patients and in emergencies. I knew how to take temperature, pulse and respiration. I'd give patients intravenous injections; I prepared and read medical diagrams.

"Then my mom (older sister) died in an accident! Everyone said she was a good person. Many people came to her burial. They showed up and kept coming. People cried. She was always willing to give. I even remember when I was very little, there was an insane woman, a *loquita* begging for food. My mom always had a container with food to give her. I had to take over the care of her son, Andrés, and his sister.

"I married at age 22 and had five consecutive children – all male – in addition to raising my sister's son and daughter. So seven in total. They were all born in Peru. I met my husband, because he was one of my sister's college teachers. I adapted so that all I did was go from work to my children. I had an aunt who helped me before I went to work.

"My husband and I divorced many years ago. I had a problem with him, because I am not one to put up with much. I can't put up with a man who cheats on me. So we divorced and I do not keep in touch. I am not sure if he remarried or even where he is living.

"My children range in age from 42 (oldest) to 36. The eldest, Yuri, lives in Spain; Yakov Moises lives in Peru and has an eight-year old daughter – my only grandchild. My son Nikolai is married and does not have any children; my son Vladimir lives in Orlando. Pavel, my youngest, lives in Arizona. All my children have been successful. They are all professionals and have their life ahead of them. One studied mechanical production; one is a pastor of a church and has written a few books. The children are now scattered - living all over the world. One is in Spain, one in Florida, one in Arizona, and two in Peru. Besides my nephew and son in the U.S., I no longer see my other children. We speak by phone, but it is different. We do not see each other anymore.

"The most important thing in my life is my children. I have struggled for them so they can do something in life. I worry that they are well. It is everything I want. Even if they do not give me anything, as long as they are okay, it is the most important thing. I wish them to have a tranquil life. If they get sick, I worry. Last month, I was concerned and nervous, because my married son, Nikolai, who lives in Lima, was in a coma from a generalized infection. I thought he would die. We're so far away, so I did not know much about the situation and no one explained it to me. His wife didn't explain it. She only told me he had a generalized infection. He took a while to come out of the coma – three months. The infection was strong and affected his throat, ears and stomach. He could not eat and was fed intravenously. But he recovered and told me 'he feels good now.'

*****

"As I said, I was not thinking of staying in the U.S. I wanted to return. But I had to stay. I have now lived in the States for 16 years. I have my Peruvian passport, but it is expired. To renew it, I need to go to the consulate in San Francisco. I pay taxes yearly. I have an ITIN number and pay tax as a self-employed person, because I am not working for a company. The IRS does not care about my immigration status, as long as I pay taxes on my wages. I do not earn much, so I will not have to pay anything extra.

"I would love to fix my immigration situation in the U.S. That way I can return to Peru. I am retired in my country. I have to go through some paper work to get my pension. I worked there for 23 years. I only needed two more years for a full pension, but they have to give me something. I have already received the documents at my house that tell me I can make withdrawals. However, I have to fix it from here. Since I haven't been able to do the paperwork, I can go to the Peruvian consulate and authorize my son that lives in Lima to take care of it. It will take about a year and a half to do it.

"I would like to live a quiet life, without problems, but things are not always so. I do not want to hurt anyone or have anyone hurt me. No harm, no evil thought for others. To want for others what I want for me. If one gets into someone else's life, you get in trouble. It brings you problems – don't intervene. Each person as they are accounts to God personally.

"My family was Christian, but we did not go to church. I started going to church, a long time ago, when I was already an adult. Now I am very religious, a Christian Apostolic. My religion helps me live peacefully. Every day the first thing when I wake up, I entrust my path to God. For him to guide my children and me. I do that every day. So my confidence comes from God. If I have problems, I pray and tell God. I trust him and the problem is solved. It is the tranquility I have because I rely on him. When my son was ill, I asked my church to pray for him. And now he's well. We leave it in God's hands, and if something does happen, then it is because he permits it. Then it was his time.

"I do not have any goals left for me. I am an old lady. I do not know if I will stay here or return to Lima. I leave it in God's hands. As he says, 'Do not think of what has to be tomorrow, because every day brings its desire.' So I think every day, my future will be whatever God chooses for me."

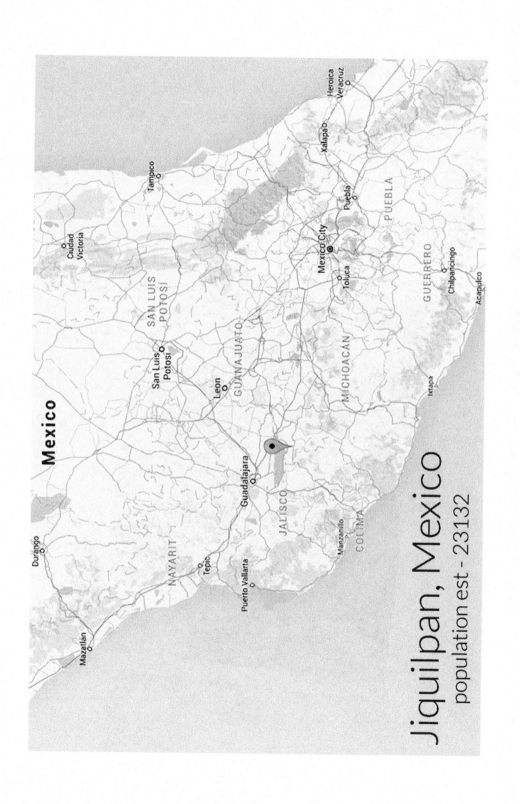

Jiquilpan, Mexico
population est - 23132

Chapter 6

José Luis's Story

"The town where I'm from, Jiquilpan in Michoacán, Mexico, is where one of the most famous presidents of Mexico was born. He was called General Lázaro Cárdenas del Río. He was famous because he took back oil wells from the United States. America used to be the owner of Mexican oil. The General knew that if he fought the United States, the U.S. was going to win. He decided to make an agreement with them. The story says that the United States government said, 'Ok, if you want it back you have to pay us something.' I do not know if it's true; it is said that the General paid with animals, oxen, cows, with chickens, with pigs, with whatever they had, to recover the oil.

"General Cárdenas del Río is famous. Many Americans might not have liked him, because it was a lot of oil. They must have thought, 'We've already taken their land, we don't want them to starve.' Then the General was respected and the oil returned.

"This president, the one that paid them, was born in the city where I was born. And it's a small town, about a quarter of a million people. Two Mexican presidents came from the town and are acknowledged by history. Two good presidents from one small town are not easy.

"In our national histories, all of our presidents have been corrupt. For example, if a president were from Colima, he would intentionally give a lot to the people of his town, his state. If a president were from Chihuahua, he'd grab money to benefit his people and make them rich. This president was asked, 'You are ending your period serving as president and what will you leave your people, if you have not done anything in your town? You have not built factories, you have not given them anything like other presidents have done.' He did not want to steal or be corrupt. He said, 'I'm going to leave something that the people are never, ever going to forget. I'll leave education for them.' He built all the best schools in the country in his city. Then others said, 'But there are no factories,' and he said, 'Yes, but the people in my village will be the ones owning the companies, managing the companies. They are the ones who will make all of you earn more money, but they will be managers.' And he did just that.

"In my town, most people are well-educated. There are many people from Michoacán who have not been to school, but there are many options to go to school there. Cárdenas built the largest technology college across the country. It included a language lab, gym, tennis, separate football fields, soccer fields, basketball, volleyball, everything, with nothing to envy from a first world school, a school similar to those found here in the U.S. - a great school. It was a finishing school, like a college, but was technological. That was what he wanted. 'I do not want my countrymen to be workers, I want them to be professionals.'

"I was born on January 7, 1963. I was named José Luis after my uncle who lives in Fresno, California. My mom was born on a ranch called La Lagunita. It's about 20 km from the village where we were born. My dad is from the same town where I was born, Jiquilpan. They were both from in the state of Michoacán. We are eight in total – two brothers, my brother and me, and six sisters.

"I didn't meet my grandfather, my dad's dad, because he died before I was born. He died in an accident - a train ran over him. He was a construction worker. The train caught him and he died. My grandmother married another man, my father's stepfather. He lived with his family, his sons. When I was growing up, we always visited them. My grandmother helped me, because I was her favorite grandchild. Secretly she was always giving me money and sometimes my cousins would ask her, 'Why? He is not even our cousin and you always give him.' 'Because he never asks for anything! You are always asking me. He comes here and does not even ask for bread.'

"My step-grandfather's name was Ramon and when he died they did not tell me until about a month after it happened, because they said, 'If we had told you, you would have wanted to come back.' He loved me more than his own children. His family went to his home only to grab things and people would say, 'You never have to watch José Luis, you don't need to watch over him.' 'No, I know, I can let him in my house and he never touches anything. I have to be careful with all the rest of you.'

"My grandmother, my mother's mother, died when she was 114 years old. She was really old. When she died the same thing happened. My mom did not tell me until after some time. When people close to me died, I used to go back home, but mainly when I was single. Sometimes. I would have had just returned to the States. 'Do not tell him, he just got back.' And they wouldn't tell me until later.

"My grandfather, my mother's father, still lives. He was younger than my grandmother who died at 114. Right now he must be around 104 years old. Do you know why? Because they live on his ranch. They live healthily. I would go to visit them and they said, 'Well, right now I'm going to make a chili.' And my grandmother would go to the back of their farm and bring onions, tomatoes, cilantro she had just harvested from her garden.

"My dad was always the type of person who worked. He was humble and honest. A word to describe him is illiterate. He never went to school. He did not study anything, but he was a very intelligent person. He could not read or write, signed with crosses and numbers, but he knew a lot. He made his own bills when he signed contracts, because he was not going to work just for the day. He had contracts to build houses. My dad was our provider. He was not a person who declared his love for others. We knew that he loved us and he made every effort to give us the best.

"One of the things I remember most about him is that when I was three years old, we lived in a poor area. It was very difficult to get by and I do not know how he managed, but he got me a tricycle. Everyone envied me and borrowed it. And mind you, rather incredibly, what one remembers when you were little and I remember when I was three. And I remember things as if I were seeing them right now, with my grandmother, my mom, and my dad. Things that happened and that stayed with me and left their marks. I remember that day my cousins were fighting to get to ride my tricycle and my mom said, 'Don't let them, they will break it.' I said, 'No, they don't have one, let them ride it.' My son now behaves like me. It was moving because, I bought a battery car for his birthday and most adults said, 'No, do not let them climb on your car, they're going to break it.' 'Why not? They are poor and they do not have money to buy one; their parents can't buy it.' I had to go buy an extra battery, because it would end up with no charge when he was playing alone.

"My mom took care of our home. She was a strong character and that was very good for us. My mom was hard with us. She'd tell us to do homework, homework, homework. To eat properly. My mom went to school for a very short time; it was like three or four years. She was of humble origin and people of her origin did not care about education. No, let us be donkeys. For them, work, work and work. No, my mom made sacrifices, washed and ironed outside the home. She'd go to work as a maid, cleaning houses to get money to give us what we needed. My dad sometimes did not make enough.

"The first memory of my childhood is sad. All the children where I lived were part of my family. Back then, everyone thought the only future was coming to the U.S. That's what they told you. If you were big and strong you would come to work here to send money to your parents. My parents saw that I was brilliant at school and I liked going to school. My mom said, 'No, if we stay here we are going to be the same, and I see you are quieter than everyone else, you do not move in the same circles as them.' So my mother convinced my father to move the family to a different town where there would be more opportunities. In the community of Jiquilpan, there was violence between the same family, domestic violence. Families are wrapped in the same problems and that's why my mom saw that she did not want to go to that extreme with my dad. She wanted to leave that place because, you know, when mothers and sisters are involved it becomes a big problem. And I saw that my dad was very different from his brothers and his family. My mom convinced him that we should move to another area.

"People in our new neighborhood were quite different from those where we lived with the family. They had also separated from those areas and wanted a different kind of life, a humble but different life. The area where we had lived was like a closed neighborhood where we all lived together. Once we moved, we lived in our own house, by ourselves. Each house was separate from the others. Humble houses, but everyone had their home.

"Sometimes it makes me sad, because you see people coming to the U.S. and one hears their stories. Many say, they came here and fell in love with an apartment because it has carpet, or because it has a bath, where one can bathe with hot water or that they have a toilet. We had all this stuff, but we did so humbly. Even though my dad never went to school, he was a successful construction worker. He made a great effort to be able to give us those things. Even if he could only afford a battered old car, we'd have a car. He made a lot of sacrifices, and my mom, too. My mom's main responsibility was to get us to stay in school and study, study, study. My dad brought in the money. We used to help in whatever we could. When we were little, I remember, there was a river near my house and to start making the foundation for our new house, we would carry stones. Everyone carried stones. At that time my siblings were tiny; the younger ones were four or five years old and they carried a pebble.

"In the area where we moved, we begin to think in a different a way. Things changed. Now it was not growing up to come to the United States, but to find a way to progress in the country. Study. School, school, school. My parents started noticing improvement with all my siblings. I was a bit better in school than others, but they sent us all to school. When they wanted to send me to a paid school, I said, 'No.' They were sacrificing too much for me. I thought we all should have the same opportunity, because we were brothers and sisters. I did not want them to continue paying for me, so I went to a public school. I thought if I wanted to go to a school farther away it would be due to my own merits. So I started making my own way. I began to excel in class. I received a full scholarship. We got free vacations all the time then and we all dedicated ourselves to studying.

"I was good at school. I mean, because my friends would say, 'Hey, but you never study and always do well.' I never liked to miss classes and I paid attention. I also practiced doing math. While listening, I was practicing and doing math and just studied the day before an exam. My strategy was that I related numbers, dates, names, everything to things. Each one of us has his own tips. I like sports; so I related it to someone or something famous. The names and dates. It was always very easy for me.

"When I was not in school or studying, I played soccer. Always. My team was called America. My dad wanted me to play baseball and that was one of our arguments, because I didn't like baseball. If I had stayed in the area, I would have played baseball, because he had bought me equipment. But I did not like baseball and the area where we moved to, we all played soccer.

"When I was young, my idea was to be a soccer player. In fact, I could have been one, if I had not come to the U.S. I had a chance to play. When I came to the U.S., I was paid to play on certain teams. I was paid for playing on teams that played well. To me, if I stayed in Mexico, I possibly could have played soccer professionally. When I got here too. To me soccer has always been a hobby. I would never say it would be my business, because I had friends who were good and ended up with some defects, or foot injuries. I thought, that's not going to sustain me for life, and I started to do other things.

"When I was on vacation from school, my dad taught me electricity. Then in the houses he built, I did the electrical installations, ever since I was very young. I was in high school and I had to do the installations. I had people working with me at that age. They would do things I could not do, such as making holes in the walls. My dad said, 'You have to pay people before you will get your money. I do the work, you get paid and you pay your people. Take the money you make, put it in the bank so you'll never have to ask us for money for school.' I never asked them for any money. Sometimes, my mom never told me, but I knew that money was tight. There was always some bill, light, water or something. Without her knowing I would get the bill paid. Later when the collectors arrived to the neighborhood, they would tell her, 'No Doña Lola, your son already came and paid the bill!' She'd scold me. 'Why? You never ask for money, you never ask!' 'No, mommy, I have what I need.'

"My dad said that since he worked in construction, he wanted me to be an engineer. That was another problem that I had with him. Engineering was well suited for people who liked to deal with numbers, like I was. However, mom wanted me to do something quieter, close to home, like being in an office or something. I did what she wanted. When I finished high school, my parents gave me as a trip to Manzanillo, Colima as a graduation gift. We had family that lived there. When I returned, my mom had enrolled me in administrative sciences. So I went, I did my tests and everything and people would tell me 'Hey! You are such a good student, you will go to waste in science, come here.' 'No, my mom says there and I'm going there because it will cost her, and I will not have much time to be working.'

"I did not go into the military. I have led a blessed life, really. When I went to submit my application, after high school, it turned out that the general of the division shared my name, José Luis. When I arrived, they said: 'You don't need to do anything.' He signed my application, and I left. It depended on the year you were born; my generation had to enroll.

"After secondary school, I attended a technological school. My favorite subject was math. I was studying for a Bachelor of Accounting. Numbers, numbers. I came up to the U.S. a year before finishing. In fact I had planned to return to finish my career, but no, I didn't do it. I was studying in the technology school. During the holidays, in 1985, my brother, who knew I was a good student, and was living here in the U.S., in California, said, 'As payment for your good grades and all your efforts, come to the U.S. Then you can earn some money for your studies, for you to continue.'

"For me, everything was fine while I studied. It was a very difficult life change to come from Mexico to the States, mainly because you live your whole life studying over there. You come here and you cannot do that, because you are old enough to work. If I had been born in the U.S., it would have been different, since I liked studying. I think I would have done something.

"It took me two days by bus to reach the border. It took two days, because the buses can only go the speed limit. I went through the hills, with a person who had an agreement with the coyotes. He was given money and asked to help people across. At that time it was cheap. He charged me roughly $300 and my crossing was easy. We went through San Ysidro, the border town near Tijuana. We were all going to go together in a car. The coyote saw us all and said to me, 'OK, you're going to go through sitting in the passenger seat of the car.' I got some glasses and I got a newspaper and I went through the line and everyone else was hidden below, inside the car. An American was driving and Immigration just said, 'Okay' as we passed. It was not very difficult. The driver just said, 'He is my friend and we came to visit' and he told me, 'Don't talk and pretend to be asleep.' And so we went through the border.

"Once I crossed, I was in San Juan Capistrano, a city near the border. When we arrived there the guy said, 'Let's eat at McDonald's' and we went to eat at McDonald's. I said, 'Hey, we better go and eat on the way, because my friends are down there in the car.' They didn't get out. They were hidden in the bottom of the car. They knew how to do it. There is a cover below, and they traveled beneath it. People cross in many different ways. I did not have to live through that. I sat, comfortably. That is how I crossed the first time.

"I came in 1985 and worked in the fields, in Santa Maria, California. I worked there for 4 or 5 months. In the field picking strawberries. It was hard work. I earned about $60 per day – they paid per box. When I went to the U.S., it was only for a period of 3 to 4 months, to earn some money and then go back to Mexico. I saw how hard the work was, so I told my brother, 'I will not return to the United States ever, because it is very hard work.' At that point I had made, for that time, a lot of money. I said to myself, 'If I ever return to the United States I'll come on a plane, not running down the hill.' I told him, 'If I come back, it'll only be on those terms.' I returned to Mexico. When I returned, I went by car with my friends. They took me by car all the way back to Michoacán. It took us around 36 hours–we all drove.

"The following year my brother said to me, 'Do you want to come back?' I was attending the technological school and I said, 'I'll only go on the conditions I said before. I do not want to go through the hills.' My brother sent me money and I went to apply for a visa at the U.S. Consulate in Guadalajara. As I was an excellent student, I applied for a student visa. I took my notes with me to the interview. I was only planning on coming to the U.S. for the holidays. I was going to go for the second time, but they did not know I had been there before. They granted me an indefinite visa, for life, as a student, but on vacation. So the second time I came to this country was in 1986 with a student visa. My brother paid for the round trip airfare. When I came here, the second time, it was easy. I arrived in Los Angeles and my family was waiting for me; my cousins, my uncles, my brother all came to fetch me at the airport. And I stayed. I did not return.

"I came to the Bay Area because my brother lived in San Jose and my cousins lived in other parts of the San Francisco Bay Area. My uncle lived close to Fresno on a ranch. The rest of my cousins lived in Los Angeles. My brother told me that there were many jobs available. I had come during my vacation time. I had only come for the holidays, really, so we went to Disneyland, to the Studios; we visited San Francisco, the Golden Gate and everything else. At that point I thought I was only staying for the holidays. Once they were over, I would return, because I had my ticket back and I was twelve months – just two semesters, away from completing my college degree. So I came and then, no. I started working and I started making money.

"People asked me, 'Why didn't you finish college?' I regret that. When I arrived in Fresno, my uncle told me, 'Go to school to learn English. Here you won't have money, but you'll have a house, and you will not pay rent.' And I ignored him, because I did not want to live on a ranch and I came over here and I can´t regret it.

"I began working in the strawberry fields again. A man who worked for the company saw me and took an interest in me. He saw I was quite different. He saw I was not dressed like the others. I wasn't wearing a hat or a cap. I looked like a city boy. He saw me and said, 'Don't you think this job is too heavy? Too rough for you?' 'Yes, but this is where I am earning my money.' 'Okay, I have an easy job for you. Do you know how to drive?' 'Yes.' Then I started to help move trucks around inside the ranch. I drove trucks and fork lifts in his cellar where fruit was stored. I started to do different activities, but not in the sun.

"When I came the second time, I stayed longer. My brother told me, 'I was making it.' This was in 1986, when Silicon Valley was strong. There was a lot of work, hard work. Back then companies were open 24 hours. You worked as long as you wanted. I worked 14 or 16 hours daily.

Then the Amnesty came. I did not know what the rules were. I found out that if I worked more than ninety days in 1986 - and yes, I had worked, around 100, 120 days, - then you qualified for amnesty. So I stayed. I already wanted to go back, but my brother said I had a chance if I stayed in the U.S.

"My parents were sad when I went to the U.S., although not at first. At first they thought I was only coming here for the holidays, and when I told my mom I was staying. My mom was always hard on us, but she was very brave in other things. I said to her, 'You know what, mom? I'll be staying there,' and she said, 'I'll feel sad, but only God knows why he does things in this way. Maybe your future is there.'

"I had complained about this country. We come here almost like slaves. I didn't like that. Then I thought, well, I'm here anyway. If I do not do well, I can return. I used to visit my friends in Los Angeles. When I went to visit them, they were working, selling hamburgers at McDonald's, in Burger King, or working in hotels. I thought, maybe this will be my future and I will end up staying here like them. My friends could not get papers and they always had to come over with a coyote. Here is my chance - because the visa I had only allowed me to come on holiday, not to work.

"My brother said, 'You have an option; you can file your paperwork. Get your green card and when you want to return to Mexico you'll be able to come and work with your papers, and forget about your visa. You'll have your papers.' I went and paid $185. This happened when Ronald Reagan was president. He was the one who established this law, the famous amnesty program. I filed my papers. At that time, the U.S. government was afraid of AIDS. It was a serious problem at the time. I had to take a test and if you tested positive they would not give you papers. I did everything. It went well and in November, 1990 I became a permanent resident.

"I met my wife, Alicia, at a party, in a dance center the first time I came to the U.S. She loved to dance. At that place, the man that received the admission tickets was from the same town as me. He invited me and I saw her and I asked her to dance with me. We started to get to know each other. She was my girlfriend and then I went back to Mexico. Then later, when I returned, we began seeing each other again. She became pregnant almost immediately. That was 19 years ago.

"In Mexico I had been married before, but it did not work. I married a girl who was an applied chemical drug biologist, the best student in the whole country. She was from my hometown and she studied at Instituto Tecnológico de Morelia, in the University of Michoacán of San Nicolas de Hidalgo. I married her when I was 25 years old. I had it all planned. I said, 'I'll have two children, a boy and a girl and I'm going to get married at 25.' And when I was 25 years old, I got married. I was used to being in the U.S. and I thought she could continue studying at any university she wanted, being an excellent student. So I said, 'Go study at Stanford, and that's where we will live.' But her family got involved and she paid more attention to her family. Her family wanted her to go to Harvard. Neither of us gave in. We had no children, we got divorced. We were legally married, but hadn't had our ceremony, yet. So the marriage got annulled, because I came here. I was going to go back to get married in church, but I didn't. We talked. We lived two completely different lives, and we would not agree on many things. We decided to cut our losses and remain friends. She still visits my family. She got married and remained friends with my mom and my sisters.

"Then I started living with Alicia. We got married after we had children, to solve her immigration status. We lived in Redwood City and eventually bought a house. My children were born in the U.S. When I was single, I went out. I was here, I was there, I had no commitments. I had girlfriends, I traveled, this and that. My life changed the day my daughter was born. When my wife became pregnant, I said, 'No!' because she was talking about having an abortion. My mom called me, because she found out. My wife had called my mom in Mexico and told her and she must have thought I was going to do what everyone does, run away. My mom told me 'No, I do not want that. If you do that, do it, but I do not want to see you at home ever again.' It wasn't necessarily that, because I still had it in my head that maybe I'd go through with it, but I wanted her to be born. She was born in Sequoia Hospital in Redwood City. When I held her for the first time, I felt moved. When I held my daughter and hugged her, there was nothing else. She is 18 years old now.

"Since my daughter was born, I changed a lot. When my friends looked for me, they would say, 'You are a wimp.' 'Well, yes I am. Look, here's the reason, my daughter!' Wherever I went, I brought my daughter. I took her everywhere. There are lots of pictures. My friends would say, 'Hey! You only live for your daughter.' 'Yes, I live for my daughter' and when I got angry with my wife and everything and she'd ask, 'Will you leave?' 'No, I will not leave because of her.' And then my son was born and my life got even better. My son will be 16. He was born two and a half years or so after my daughter.

"When my daughter was in elementary school, she started liking numbers. 'But how will I do it daddy?' At that time we rented a large house in Redwood City. I used some big cardboard signs to make the multiplication tables. It's not very common here and I wore them and said, 'Review them.' Tables from 1 to 10 and from 1x1, 9x7, and so on. She advanced a lot in math after that. My son does not like it. My son had a problem at birth. He almost died. He pooped when he was about to be born, something got to his head. But it's okay. It's not bad, but it takes him longer to remember things. He just needs helpful tips. For the things he likes, he has learned everything without problem. He likes soccer and knows all the names and everything there is to know of all the teams worldwide. Whatever he is interested in, he knows perfectly. But things like math and school in general - not so much. When you push him a little, he moves forward. He'll say, 'You know what Daddy? I want these tennis shoes, but they cost this much.' I respond, 'I have no money now to pay for them. We will calculate the card payments, but you have to promise me that you'll do better, because I see that you are not doing well in school.' After some time he'll come back and say, 'No, on these I did great, here is this one' and shows me. My wife scolds him. She is stronger but does not know how to read or write. I'd tell her, 'Leave him. He made an effort, and we will not punish him.' She says to him, 'No, but look at your sister, how excellent she's doing.' 'No, no, shut up with that! No, you can't say something like that.'

"My daughter makes me proud. It is said that genes are inherited and I think she has inherited my genes. Of course, everyone speaks the best about their children. My children are very noble. When I do well here, when they are going somewhere, I say, 'Do you need money?' And they are not like other kids that always want money. They'll answer, 'I don't need any, I still have some.' They are honest; they are noble. I am proud of that. I do not treat them as if I were a general or anything. My wife is harder on them, but I am not. Everyone is educated differently, because my wife wants things exactly as she says. I like freedom; they decide for themselves, but of course, one tries to teach them the things that you think are not appropriate on the way. I trust my children, because I have taught them. Even when something bad happens, nothing matters. If it's something they broke, we will repair it. We can deal with anything; we don't need to hide anything.

"I like to be organized. Sometimes people say, 'You have everything written down, all that you need to do every day.' I just like to be organized with my stuff, and I try to do it at home with my children, but children don't. They get into their rooms and make a mess. I say, 'Go tidy your room,' because sometimes my son makes a mess in his room; my daughter leaves her shoes in the bathroom or leaves a shirt on our bed. 'Try to be organized.' My wife argues with our children and I tell her, 'You know what? Do not get upset. Shut the door and do not look inside. They'll have to clean it up when it's their turn.' They clean up each week. I try to be quiet, calm, because I've seen things I would not like them to go through. I try to be patient with them as much as I can.

"I'm also very practical. For example, my daughter started driving. She gives everyone rides and I say, 'You know Sandra, don't give rides to everyone, because people will get used to it, and everyone will start asking you to do it, and when you don't have time people will think you are mean for saying no.' It's happening. 'Daddy, you told me this would happen.' 'I just told you, now you're seeing it for yourself.'

"I want my children to study as much as they can. My daughter may go to Foothill College. She has not decided yet. She has a few options. She wants to go to Texas and has a scholarship to go there. She also likes another school in Monterey; I'd like that, it's closer. What I tell her is that if she likes numbers she should look for something related to them. It seems as if she likes dentistry, because I see her books and they are related to that. My son wants to be an athlete, but he is not very dedicated. I have to be more careful with him, because he is very attached to home. I feel he has slightly less capacity for school. Especially if he is not so good at something, you at least have to dedicate your time to do that and not other things. He doesn't like school, and then they start doing other things, wandering the streets. Watching them grow and seeing that they stay on track, is very important to me. I am aware, especially in this age, it is important to know what they are doing, especially with their friends, because that's where they deviate. I live to see my children grow up.

"While my children had been growing up, I first worked in assembly in the company Zircon where my brother worked. I stayed there for 5 years and then the company relocated to Mexico. Then I worked in a similar position for three years at Qualtronics. And then for a company called GM Resound. They made devices for people who could not hear well. I tested the devices with a computer. I ran a test to see if they were working well, to send them to the client. But the company moved to Minnesota - it used to be in Redwood City – and my wife did not want to move with the company. And so we stayed in Redwood City. That decision greatly affected our lives.

"It was a good job and after we chose not to move with the company, I could not find another job like that one. Then we lost everything. We lost our house when the economic crisis came. We had been paying for the house for six years. We lost it when I lost my job and my wife was deported. We had no money to pay. My work decreased a lot. We were living on unemployment and things got ugly. We had to move to a place where we'd pay less. Once we moved, it wasn't so bad and after some time I thought, it's better this way. We were just thinking about the mortgage payment all the time and we confined ourselves, and those who were suffering the most were my children. There was no money for eating out, no money for McDonald's and we couldn't go to Great America. Everything had stopped because of the house payment. When we ended up losing the house, it took the stress off. We couldn't even have lunch out. Everything had to be cooked at home and everything we bought was the cheapest we could find. After we moved out of the house, I knew what we had to pay. We had more possibilities to do more things. We started to rent and now we rent an apartment belonging to a church in San Jose. The apartment has two bedrooms and cost about $1,200 per month.

"After losing the house I began drinking a lot. Once, I saw that my son was hiding because he could see how wasted I was. That's the saddest thing - I remember that. When I was into the habit of drinking, I got as far as going to the street and wanting to live in my car for a while. People came to find me, 'You don't need to be like this.' My brother gave me phones twice, to be able to communicate with me, and I lost them. I did not want to know anything about anyone. I just wanted to be there, doing that. I realized if I carried on in this way I would lose my family, I would lose everything. Not my family - my children, what is most important to me.

"Like I said, after we lost our house, I began to drink a lot. Eventually, I went to the Victory Outreach Rehabilitation Center for 10 months. After I came out, I came to the Day Worker Center, because I had friends there – I knew Mauricio and Francisco from Venezuela. I met them while I was in the rehabilitation center. I was about to begin looking for a job, but I went to the Center to look for them. When I came to the Day Worker Center to look for them, I talked to one of the people that worked for the Center. I told her I'd I come to look for my friends and she said, 'But then do not go looking for work - why don't you fill in an application?' 'Okay, I'll fill one in just in case.' I did not find my friends that day. The next day I came back. I intended to just go and visit. I just wanted to see them and greet them and ask for their phone numbers. But when I came the next day the Center asked me, 'Do you want to go to work? You will make more or less this much, for about three or four hours.' And I said, 'Well, I can do this while I wait for my friends to return from their jobs.' I worked, and decided to stay. It is two years since I came here. It has been since then that I have not done taxes because I did not know what records they kept at the Center and I thought I just had to ask for them, but I couldn't. I did not know how all of this was handled. This year I'll be a little more prepared.

"At the Center, I work at whatever happens to come my way. Whatever is offered. If there's moving, gardening, anything. It's manual labor more than anything. The Center sometimes has a little more appreciation for me on some things. For example, in organizing the work. Almost always, if we're three or four workers, I get the instructions and deliver them to others. Tell them what they will have to do. No, I cannot do any electrical work, because is a bit different here than it was in Mexico. The materials, especially the type of construction and everything. It's not that hard, actually; I just need to catch up. I would like to do something like that in the future. Because an electrician is well paid. At our home I used to do some electrical work, but not now since we rent.

"Yesterday, Sunday, there was a job through the Center, and the director, was a little annoyed at me; she said, 'Hey, there's that work,' and I said, 'I always go to work, but only eight hours on a Sunday.' It had been already three Sundays that I had not been with my son. 'I will not ask him,' I told the director. I couldn't. I can work 8 hours, but starting early. The other day I was at this event for more than 16 hours from 9:00 a.m. to 3:00/4:00 a.m. in the morning the next day. But it's money. Money is necessary; but sometimes ... there are other important things too – like watching soccer with my son.

"I come to the Day Worker Center because I don't have any other work. There are a few citizens at the Center. I have my application on Call Jobs. I've been to interviews, but they do not call me. I think it is because of what I'm looking for - because on my resume there is the kind of work I actually do. These jobs are new to me. Physical work is new for me. My previous jobs were doing the kind of work that was not as hard. I have a lot of experience with electronic assembly. Some companies have called me, but I go and do the test, and then, as usual, 'We'll call,' and they do not call me. I'm hopeful, maybe, you never know. I went all the way to Hayward and Fremont, where most of these companies are now located. I have a lot of experience in assembly, especially welding. I know it's difficult, because all those jobs have been taken, and are being done in other countries. I do want one of those jobs so that I can have my 40 hours. It is more stable.

"Even though I have lived here for more than 24 years, I have not become a citizen. I have to do that, but have not because I haven't filed taxes in the last few years. I have not filed because I've only had jobs like this – day labor jobs. That's the problem. I paid taxes for many years and I only owe the last three years. I need to get a lawyer and tell him about my situation. That's what I intend to do, but I have not done it yet because of the economy. It would cost about $600; that is not much in itself, if you are single and living alone. I can come up with the money, but the problem is that I have my family. I have my daughter, my son, my wife, and I have to contribute to pay our expenses. I can't, I can't. That's why I have not done it yet, but my record is not bad. I could do it. I have always filed tax returns. Because I made very little, I always got refunds of up to $8,000. I did not include, as many who do not have papers do, many dependents. The government does not return almost anything in that case. I included only myself and one dependent. So I got money returned.

"Now that I'm living life differently, I do not need other things to be okay. I'm glad I found that out. I always say people here get materialistic, thinking only about the money, and I do not think in the same way. I sometimes have arguments with my wife because she is thinking about money all the time. I say that, because I am comfortable. When it's Father's Day, my son will come and tell me, 'Here Daddy, I don't have anything else to give. I know, you do not work.' And he'll give me a card, and it's worth more than anything to me.

"I have good memories of Mexico. Although I still have a little anger against my dad because my dad left my mom when we were older. I do not know, in the end I cannot say if it was a bad thing to do. Each person has his own thoughts - but he left my mom. My mom gave him all the best years in her life and everything. Women like those you cannot find anymore, a woman of only one man. She stayed at home and he went away. He wanted part of the house and everything. We all had to provide a little money to give to him so that he'd leave my mother alone. My mom stayed in his house.

"My brother, my cousins all live here in the States. We all send my mom money. She doesn't really need much, but still. For her to pamper herself once in a while. I send her what I can, depending on how I do here. At least $100 per month, that's what I can send her most of the time. My mom still lives in our house. She does not want come to live here. She has her visa. She comes to visit twice a year, but it is hard for her because she has to travel. When she comes here, she has to visit her children in Los Angeles, Modesto, Hayward, San Jose and New York. We can meet here. But she has to travel to Los Angeles and then to New York. If she has enough time she'll visit all three places. We each have to pay for her to travel to our house.

"Before, I was the one that was better off, economically, than everyone else in my family. I had good jobs and everything. But when everything slowed down, I did not follow the company that hired me, because of lack of support from my wife. But anyway, we are all here and everything is good. Economically everyone is able to bring my mom over whenever they want. I am the only one who can't. That is why I give her some money each month. She does not want to live here. She is at home and at home is where she wants to be. Someday I'd like to reunite everyone. Sometimes I think, 'If one day I hit the lottery', which is the only way I would be able to have enough money, I would buy a home and we would all live there, my whole family.

"I'll be honest - It's hard. Here, in the Day Worker Center, most people are alone; many have wives in Mexico. I live with my wife. We don't have a good relationship, and sometimes we have problems - she is very difficult. There have been occasions when I've left home. It is very difficult when you know that they are doing something wrong and they say, 'I know I'm doing something wrong, but that's me and I will not change.' You can't do anything with that. I said, I'd stop drinking, but she has a problem also ... she loves casinos. You can't get her out of there. She wanted us to live in Las Vegas. I have an aunt in Las Vegas who offered us a studio and she said, 'Let's go there.' I told her, 'No, I do not want to go to Las Vegas, because you won't be able to get out of the casinos; if we move there it is going to be worse.'

"Maybe, taking refuge in this I'll go back to drinking. Right now I'm fine and calm, without doing so. I have spent almost three years without drinking. I did it alone. I walked away from where Mauricio and Francisco were, and I did it for me. I lasted 10 months in rehabilitation, and I kept thinking... 'My children need me, need my money, whatever I can give them. I'm going home.' I've kept myself sober without going to those places. I haven't even gone back to church.

"I believe in God. I like to meditate. Occasionally, I go to church. I have no specific religion. I've been through Catholicism and other forms of Christianity. To me, God is only one, and he is where you go and is with you always. Everything depends on how you fulfill your commandments. To me, the most important book in church is the commandments. If you try to respect them, to the best of your abilities, it will show you a good path.

"Even after all the errors I've made, I consider myself a person who has not made mistakes. I do not say, 'I regret this or I am ashamed of this.' In truth, even though one sometimes might say, 'Oh, I am ashamed of this,' or 'I feel bad', it is not so. If you start thinking that way, you start doing it to yourself and you'll end up traumatized. Even right now, when I'm riding the bus, people would come to me and say, 'Hey, but if you have a car, why are you standing there waiting for the bus?' 'Because I am now living my life in this way and I feel comfortable this way.'

"I have always been a peaceful person. There are people who still appreciate me because of it. I've been involved in trouble and everything and through dialogue I have avoided problems. There have been people, for example, that would have fought and I told them, 'You know what?' Talk, talk, and this can be arranged, because sometimes it is only gossip or this or that or there are misunderstandings about everything or sometimes they are drinking or something and I always avoided fights. A person that knew me used to say, 'Is José Luis here?' 'Yes.' 'There will be no fights, he convinces them, and they do not fight.' Sometimes they even talk until they end up embracing each other. These are misunderstandings; there is nothing to be fighting about. Lately I told someone, 'Okay, remember, as things stand, if there is a dispute, you'll have problems. You will have a problem, end up in court, and if the police come, you will end up in jail or deported. That's how it's going to end, and remember that you have your commitments!' 'Oh, yes, you are right - just talking.'

"I wonder how I will be remembered. I would like to be thought of as a quiet person, who makes common sense of things. Right now, what worries me the most is our economy. Sometimes there is not enough. Sometimes I get home and did well. But something always comes up. Like now, the rent increased $200. Because supposedly the church is going to make some repairs - so they say. I had already planned something, and I had told my son, 'Mexico will play against Chile in the next few days and we're going to watch the game together.' But with this increase, 'Forget about the game.' Our plans get changed."

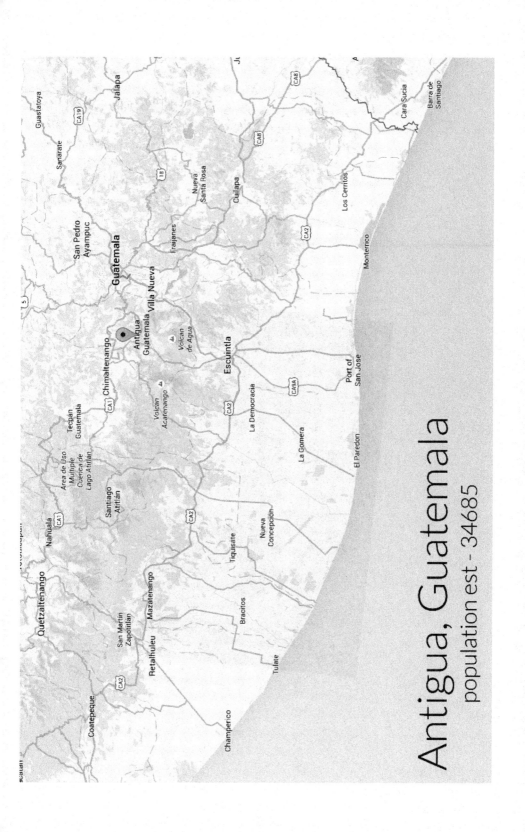

Antigua, Guatemala

population est - 34685

Chapter 7

Laura's Story

"I came to the United States from Antigua, Guatemala with a tourist visa. I brought my six-year-old daughter María Belén with me. I decided to quit my job and leave everything I had in Guatemala and come to the U.S.

"The process to obtain a U.S. visa is very difficult; they have many requirements. You have to own property: a home, a car, have a bank account and have economic solvency, in order to show that you can pay for your expenses in the United States. First, you make a phone call to the embassy to make an appointment. They then give you an appointment about a month later. After that month has passed you go to the appointment. Once in the embassy, you have to pay. When I got my visa, 10 years ago, I paid 1200 *quetzales*, (about $170). The type of visa you get depends on your financial status. Some get it for five years, others for 10 years, others are granted a visa indefinitely. My visa expires in 2018, but is only good to visit the U.S. for six months at a time - and then I need to return to Guatemala. But I am planning to stay – I do not intend to return.

"I had a good job in Guatemala. I worked in security, for the Vice-President of the country. Since I was working for the Guatemalan government, my employer handled all the paperwork for the visa. I used to travel a lot with the Vice President.

"The organization I worked for is called 'SAAS' - Secretary of Administrative Affairs and Security of the Presidency. Earlier, in 1996, peace agreements were signed in Guatemala. There are versions that say that there was a genocide, others that state there was no genocide. Before the Peace Accords were signed in Guatemala, the State, which was the army, was the one who protected the president of Guatemala. When peace was signed, the army was removed from that function and the SAAS was funded. They no longer wanted the military to look after the president, so trained civilians were assigned the job. So, that's where I started, where I began. I had no previous training; they trained me. It was a year-long intensive training, and in the process, I have protected first ladies, daughters of presidents, government ministers. I have protected both men and women. I was always a bodyguard. I have been doing this for 14 years.

"It was great. I liked my job very much, because I got to know a lot of people. You learn many things, and that never gets boring. You have no idea who you might meet that day, or where you're going. They give you the agenda the day before and say, 'Tomorrow there will be an interview at this hotel, with the Vice President, the President ...' or 'We're going to San Marcos, traveling with the first lady to give toys to children ...'

"Usually things went fairly smoothly. But once, in the area of Panajachel, a very beautiful lake in Guatemala, we had a bad experience. The first lady was coming to Panajachel the following day. I was in the advance department, and we came before and prepared everything. We would take a look at the road, determined where she was going to sit, who would be next to her, if she was going to receive a souvenir or a gift. We checked and organized all these things before she arrived.

"That day, we were in three cars, and were not wearing the suits we usually wear, because this was the day before the arrival. We would wear the suits the following day. We were armed with guns and everything, though. Then, halfway there, we had to board the cars onto a ferry to cross the lake. We did not want to board cars, because we had many things on them, even the dogs, the K9 unit and other things that we were using, for example, the white paint to make a heliport for our helicopter to land. So we didn't want to go by ferry, and decided to go around the lake, by land. We were on our trip when three men appeared in the middle of the road, standing in front of our cars, wearing ski masks, dressed as military and wearing hats so that we could only see their eyes. They were armed with AK-47s. We knew what weapons they had, because we were trained on weapons. They did not say anything to us. They thought we were tourists, because many Americans go through there, and these men steal their cameras. They use AK-47s to frighten, to intimidate. Many times they had no ammunition and after robbing people, run away towards the banks of the ravine. But on that occasion, they shot at us first. I was in the first car, so I saw them head on. They started firing, and my partner was the first to shoot back. He made me react. We got our guns out and started shooting. We got out of the car and started chasing them on foot. We found their safety area - they had food there, and even had a place to store things. We found things there, but we couldn't catch them. These men knew the area perfectly and knew where to hide. We didn't. That same day we notified the authorities of SAAS, so that the next day they had assigned people from the military to guard the perimeter of the road.

"Depending on the person I was protecting, they'd allow me to enter their house. When the person trusted me, and I had many that did, I was allowed to be inside. They even gave me a room to stay in. Those allowed inside the house were usually the kitchen crew and me. Then, when the Vice President needed something, she would say, for example, 'I need you to go buy this.' She would just say it to me, and then I would have to send someone. I received the orders and then, in turn, coordinated the staff that was outside the house. I also learned to cook and make desserts while I was working. The cooks that worked for the people I protected, taught me on the job.

"My problem is that I had a partner, my ex-husband, who was violent. He has a military career, and also has a career as a lawyer. I met him when I worked in security. He was from Escuintla, Guatemala. I married at age 21 and was married for 16 years. We had two daughters, born eleven years apart. I liked being a mother - it is exhausting but rewarding.

"The life that we had together was very good. We both worked for the government; the two of us had a good salary and we traveled a lot. I know all of Guatemala, the whole of Guatemala City and every town and city within Guatemala. We lived very comfortably with only one child. I felt that I was old. In Guatemala people get married at a very young age. Not here. Here it is very different. I was 32 years old, and I said, 'I'm old; let's decide to have one more child and I'll get an operation. We can only have one more, because I'm too old.' And then we had another baby. The fact is that we traveled a lot for work, and we didn't have more time to dedicate to more children.

"But then, my husband met a young lady, very pretty, much younger than me. He fell in love. He changed a lot, and went so far as to hit me. He was not like this before, never in his life had he hit me before. During that time, I reported him twice in for violence. I never went to the hospital for that, because the hospital that we went to was a military hospital; it would have been a problem for him. I did not want him to get in trouble, because I wanted to get a pension from him.

"I have physically endured violence with my ex-husband and in my job. However, I feel what hurt me the most is the verbal violence. Because words affect you a lot. I cried a lot, for a long time. I thought that I was to blame. My self-esteem was very low, and I went through a very difficult situation. I tried to be strong for my daughters. I tried not to show them the pain I was going through. When I was not feeling well, when I felt my self-esteem decline, I could just go to the salon and lift myself up again. But it took time for me to say, 'I can no longer deal with this life.'

"I lodged two complaints about my situation. Both reports were discarded halfway through, because my husband was a friend of the judge; he was friendly with those who handled the case. My reports were dismissed - they didn't follow them through. That was the end of the relationship, when everything finally broke. I got tired and I found no other way, so I divorced and came here. I just left. I have been divorced 3 ½ years. I never got a pension.

"The justice system in Guatemala relies heavily on corruption. If you have money, and you have power, which is the driving force in Guatemala, you can have a case. If you are just one more of the common people and have no power or powerful friends, then the justice system will not do anything for you. My ex-husband has a tourist visa and he can travel and he can be armed. He can come and go. In fact he has. But he does not know I'm in California; he knows I'm in the US, but not where I am. He is interested in finding me; he has tried to contact me, but I don't want to talk to him. I don't know if he remarried or not. I know nothing about his life; I do not care.

"The difficult thing is that I think many men cheat on women. I don't know if it happens here, but at least in Guatemala. And sometimes women forgive them. But I felt I had the means to sustain my daughters, go to the beauty salon, grab my car and go to the beach. I had independence. So I did not have to suffer him hitting me. I did not have to endure him coming home with another woman's smell. I had no reason to put up with that. I am a strong woman.

"In Guatemala, if I had had any other job, if I didn't work for the government, it would have not given me the economic solvency to provide for my daughters. I have two daughters. My husband doesn't pay any alimony. There is no child support there, as there is here. The laws in Guatemala are different. If you have the means, raising children anywhere in the world it can be easy.

"When I left my country, I flew from Guatemala to Denver; I went looking for my dad, who lived in Colorado – I will tell you about him later. Then from Denver I flew to San Francisco. I didn't like the climate in Denver. I do not like snow. I didn't enjoy the weather. And it is harder to find a job in Denver - there are more Americans than Latinos. When I was in Denver, I could barely speak and communicate with people, because they all speak English.

"I decided to come to the San Francisco Bay Area. I had already been here - I had traveled here before, as a tourist, for a week or two, with my bosses. There is a big Latino community here. It felt great that in stores you can be assisted in Spanish.

"As I told you, I managed to come here with my little girl, on a visa. It was a blessing that I could bring her with me, because many people don't have their children here. They wish to bring them. My oldest daughter, Camilla Inez, was 18 years old and stayed in Guatemala. She lives on the university campus. She stays at my mom's house on weekends She is studying industrial engineering, in Guatemala, in a private university and is in her third year. She only has two years left to finish college. She is very smart and loves math, like I did. She already knows more than me. Since she attends a private university, I also had to pay for her tuition.

"The situation was very hard when I arrived in the United States. I did not have a job with which I could afford food, clothing and all our expenses. I did not know the rent would be so expensive here in the Bay Area. And then my daughter, María Belén, got sick. She got pneumonia; she had a terrible cough and started coughing a lot. I took her to the doctor and they prescribed an antibiotic for her, but the antibiotic did nothing. Then it got worse. She started coughing blood, and her nose started bleeding; she developed a high fever. And I had to work. I have no family here, and I had just arrived. I had no friends or acquaintances at that point. I had no one to leave her with and the people I usually took her to said, 'She can't come here today, she is ill and she might be contagious. She might get other children sick.' I couldn't work, I had to look after her and it was very difficult. I then decided to send her back to Guatemala to live with my mother. My daughter returned to Antigua and likes living with my mother. She misses me and misses my cooking.

"She is healthy now, but I miss her like crazy. I hope I can bring her back here later on if things are better. That is what gives me courage, strength. I hope I eventually get a stable job here, get settled so that she can return.

"I ignorantly thought I was safe here in the States. Nothing bad ever happened to me in Guatemala. I came here, and in two and a half months, I have suffered two robberies here in the U.S. First, I bought a bike to move around; I left it locked outside of my work, and when I got back the bike was gone. People say that Guatemala is dangerous, but nothing of mine ever got stolen there.

"The second robbery happened when I accompanied a woman, my landlady, to East Palo Alto. There were a lot of dark people there. The landlady had to meet with a lawyer, so we went there, because there's something like a communication center for lawyers. I was filling out a job application, and she said, 'If you want to, you can stay in McDonald's, because there is WI-FI there.' Well, I was there in McDonald's while she went to fill out the paperwork she needed, and she said, 'I will pick you up.' I put my computer on the table; I finished my application and closed it. I was then checking my phone and a dark-haired boy approached me and said, 'You running fast?' And I said, 'Yes, I'm running fast.' Then he said, 'I do not think so,' and he grabbed my computer and ran away.

"I'm still upset about the theft and my child, and because I feel that in Guatemala I had a good life. I had my house and my car. Here I have no car. I have no house, and my daughters are my main concern. I do not like living here in the U.S. I do not like that rent is so expensive, and for that reason I have to share a home. You cannot come and rent an apartment for yourself, or your family. That was one of my biggest fears also when my daughter was with me, because you share a place with people you don't know, and when you have a 6 year old girl ... But for working, there's a lot of job opportunities here.

*****

"I was born on September 24, 1975 in Guatemala City, the capital of Guatemala. I grew up in a big house - It had 7 bedrooms, two bathrooms. I lived in an area of the capital city, a nice area with my parents, who were born in San Marcos, Guatemala. My grandparents also lived in San Marcos. We went from Guatemala to San Marcos to visit them often. They had a business, a grocery shop. I loved going there with my brothers, because we used to eat things from the store, sweets.

"My dad worked in a hosiery company, called Nylon Tex. He did that and also sold cement, pebbles, sand ... building materials. He had his own business. My mother took care of the business. On weekends, my dad determined what was missing in the business and would bring it.

"My parents bought the house I grew up in. It was a nice home; it was home with principles. I have no sisters but I have 3 brothers. My parents treated all four of us equally. We all had to help around the house; we all had chores; girls and boys equally, everyone had a job.

"But then my dad came to U.S. with the idea of starting a business to help the family. But while he was in the U.S – in Denver Colorado, my dad fell in love with another woman and got married. He never returned to Guatemala, even though he can travel - he is a U.S. resident. I was 14 years old when my dad came to the States, which was a very difficult stage of my life. I was the only girl in the family and my dad loved me. He protected me more than my brothers. Then when he came here, I cried a lot for my dad. My parents haven't gotten a divorce, but they've been separated for 30 years. The lady he lives with is from El Salvador. They have visited El Salvador, but not Guatemala.

"After my father left, my home as I knew it disintegrated. My mother sold the house where we lived and we moved to a small house in Antigua, Guatemala. Our neighborhood was very quiet. They were simple, humble, ordinary houses. We could play outside, around the block, with the other children in the neighborhood. There was none of today's technology, of course. I thought it was weird, because I didn't have any sisters, I only had brothers. During Christmas or for birthdays I got dolls; I wouldn't even take them out of their boxes, I liked them but I was not interested in playing with them. I had three brothers, and when they were playing with their remote control cars and racing, I always wanted to play with them.

"Two of my three brothers stayed in Guatemala. The oldest, Alejandro, lives in Zacatecas, Mexico. He is 40 years old; we are two years apart. After me, is my brother Gonzalo who lives in Antigua, Guatemala. He is married and has a family. The youngest brother is called Daniel. He also lives in Antigua. I used to live in Antigua, near the entrance to the city, but now I live in California. The two brothers that live in Guatemala are in the army; they are military officers. One of my brothers, the one that comes after me, Gonzalo, is still guarding the President's son. The other one, Daniel, was recognized as outstanding and is sent to different provinces for 20 days at a time. He then returns home for a week and then goes back. He commands a platoon of over 30 soldiers.

"I have a bachelor's degree in electricity and am an electronics expert. Both in electricity and electronics. I had many colleagues, but I was the only woman. I have seen that women here learn a bit about electronics in high school, but in Guatemala it was rare, unusual. I was the only woman and had about 60 male classmates. I was a good student - I did well. I liked math and electronics takes a lot of math skills, like linear algebraic equations. I also completed 6 semesters of law school. I did not finish. I had two years left. I left because I could not pay for college.

"I dreamed of becoming a professional person, and have a nice, stable, safe home, and have a normal family, with a husband and children. When I came here I felt very alone. I had some money, and thought I would rent an apartment for my daughter and me, but all I could rent was a room. We found where to stay right away. I cried because I did not like the family that we lived with. In the laundries there are ads: 'Room for rent,' 'Living room for rent' or 'Shared room' without knowing anyone, and I thought, 'I must find a place to rent.' I saw the ads in the local laundromat and I immediately rented a place. And the family that lived there with me, the men drank a lot and the lady hit her children. It was a horrible environment, and I did not like it there. I did not like it, but you do not know the people you rent from.

"It was very ugly, especially the first night, because I had not brought enough blankets; I had a blanket, but it was very cold, we suffered the cold. I put a lot of sweaters on my daughter. Then I moved because I did not like it there. I moved about two weeks later. Now I share an apartment on a street behind Target. I live with a lady from El Salvador and a lady from Mexico. It is a three-bedroom 2-bath apartment. I have my own room and share the bathrooms and kitchen. I have to pay $600 per month in rent.

"After I arrived, I had to walk, and look for work, and look for any opportunities. We were hungry. I was filling out applications - nowadays everything is online. Since I did not have a computer, I went to the library, and in the library, a lady told me, 'You must go to the Day Worker Center, and they can help you find a job.'

"When my daughter came here for a month, she went to school, to Castro School. When I was looking for a school, I met three women. They had a car but they did not drive. I can drive, but I had no car. Latina women who know how to drive have learned here; I learned in my country. I can also ride motorcycles, and most women here can't.

"I will do anything here to get by. I don't look for work that I like; I look for anything I can get. Now I clean houses, and in the evenings I work in Safeway and in Target from 3:00 a.m. to 7:00 a.m. and then I come to the Day Worker Center. In Target I work restocking products. I get paid $10.55 per hour. At Safeway, I help with packing at the register, like the work little children do and get paid $10.00 per hour. I do not have a social security number but I have an ITIN number from the IRS. Every check I receive from Target or Safeway has taxes deducted from it. I send $200 each week to my mother for my daughter. Sending my daughters money and my rent are my two main expenses.

"At the Day Worker Center, you get a number every day. You have to be consistent and come all week. If you went out to work today, you go to the back of the line, and you're last the next day. And tomorrow, if there is only work for two people, only those with the number one and two get it. Even if they come in late. When I started coming here I thought, 'The early bird God helps' and I would arrive here at 7:00 a.m. But it was not true; the one with the number got the job. Typically, in a week, you can work two times through the Day Worker Center. In general the work for women is housecleaning.

"There was a day at the Center when someone came in to ask for someone who could sew. They needed to make some things for horses or ponies, some flags or pennants for horses. You had to know how to use a sewing machine. Of the women at the Center, no one knew how to operate a sewing machine – but I knew. So I went, and I had gone to work a day earlier, so in that case I was lucky. Because I knew how to sew.

"I have two days off in both jobs at Target and Safeway. I have Monday and Thursday. On Monday and Thursday I clean houses. So people look at me there in Safeway ask me, 'You work here, how did you get this job?' It is not usual. And I work with my given name. I know it is unusual, many people here told me. Many Latinos, who have seen me here in the Center, have told me that. In both places, at the entrance, there was a sign saying, 'Now Hiring.' Inside Target there are a few computers, and I applied there. I believe I was I hired because I knew some English, and because I was better educated; many immigrant women never went to school.

"Now that I am settled, I have a bit more time. I start in the afternoon, at 4:00 p.m., at Safeway, and at 3:00 a.m. in Target. Then during the day, if I have time, I take advantage and come to the Day Worker Center. I have acquaintances there, but not friends who I trust. I really like the English classes in the Center because that is a way of investing my time. If I'm not in English class, I'm cleaning houses. But I don't have any free time to go and have fun. I cannot go amuse myself if my daughters are over there. I'm better now, but do not have any friends. But I do not mind so much, because I just arrive home after work and I go to sleep.

And I do not have to worry about going to work and my child staying in the apartment alone.

"Every morning and every night, I pray for my children. I call my daughters every day. I want them to have a good family, and a nice home. I would just like to be with my daughters; I do not care if it's here or there. I do not want to be there and be miserable, and I do not want to bring them here to suffer. My desire is to do well, nothing fancy, just well. To be able to provide for them.

"After my divorce In Guatemala, there were two men who tried to get closer to me; but I would not accept anything because my children are small. I said, 'First I will get my daughters through this, and then I will see what I will do with my life.' I may marry again. Maybe. When I came here, I felt very alone. I saw that life is much easier as a couple, because if you are married, the husband pays the bills and the wife helps with the food, the clothing, etc. I am by myself... I need someone to help me and support me.

"I would like to stay in the States long enough to raise money to return home to Antigua and start a business. People have told me, 'This country is the land of opportunity.' I still have not seen the opportunities. I want to learn to be a barista, because once I save enough money here, I want to go back to my country and own a bar.

"But I would like to stay in the U.S., if I could become legal. My father, who has legal status, could help me, but I do not know how he can do that. He doesn't know either, even though he has been here for a long time. At least I have learned some English, if only by ear. I do not speak well in past / present / future verb forms, but as little as I know, my dad knows less. He came here when he was older than me, and he never worried about learning English. So he's here, living as though he was undocumented, afraid. But he has a green card. My father told me that if I could, I should find out what can be done; I should get a lawyer, which is what we'd need for him to apply for my green card.

"Well, to go to a lawyer I need money; I do not have any money. I told my situation to the Day Worker Center staff and they gave me the address of a lawyer, who was here in Mt. View, California. When I went, there was no one there. I was sent to Milpitas, where the lawyer had moved. In Milpitas I was told that they didn't cover domestic violence, and they sent me to another place. Then I went to that other place ... I have gone to several places.

"But I am only asking about my situation and not involving my father. I am not going through my dad. After that, I went to another lawyer at Stanford. But they only help you when you are already being deported, so they did not take my case, not if INS isn't already involved. So I have to wait for INS to try and deport me.

"I worked in Guatemala for 14 years and I only had a year to go in order to apply for a pension. With 10 years working in the government you already get half a pension. I can already count on that when I turn 50. But if I return now, and work for another year, I can retire for time worked and not by age. I think in the future, when I become a senior, I hope to be doing well, because I've already worked. I won't have to bother my daughters. If they want to help me, that is fine, but I will not depend on them.

"For my future life, I do not have any concerns. I am concerned about the lives of my children. María Belén has been affected by many changes, the divorce, and then I foolishly brought her over here, to do nothing but suffer. I know this change is very difficult for her. But she is very intelligent. She was only here for a month, and she learned many English words.

"Life has taught me to be very independent. I trust that I can do it, too. 'Come on! You have to work, do something with your life.' I used to exercise a lot in Guatemala. Here I've been eating a lot. I have a lot of anxiety. I cannot sit still. If I have free time, I will run; I like running, sports, and filling out applications ... moving. I want to be an example for other women, and for other women to look at me and say, 'Yes, I can do it.'"

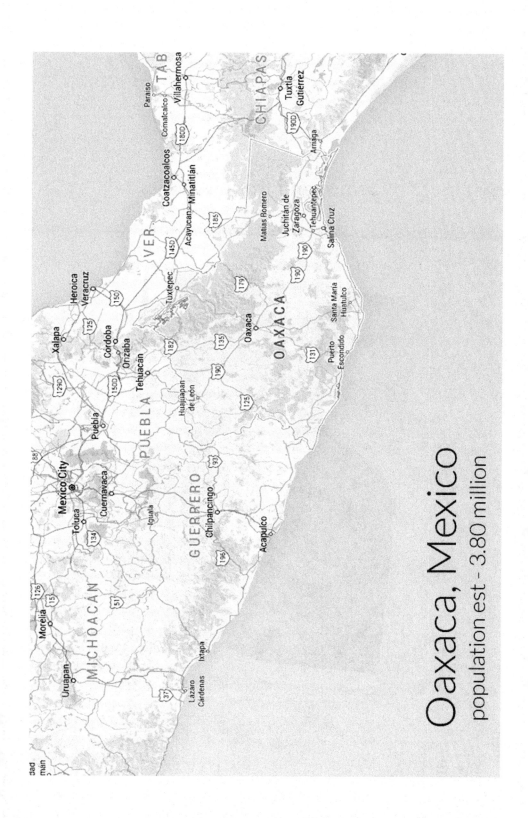

Oaxaca, Mexico
population est - 3.80 million

Chapter 8

Carmen and Rocío's Stories

Carmen

"I have two daughters. The oldest is my adopted daughter - Carmen Rojas. When I was 16, I spent four years working in the fields in Oaxaca, Mexico, planting corn, chilies and tomatoes. I met the Rojas family then - we were neighbors. Of course, I did not suspect that years later, I would adopt their daughter, Carmen, as my own. There is a lot of violence in Mexico. People steal - money, girls, livestock and property. These people killed her mom when Carmen was a young adult. But she hid in the mountains, and stayed hidden for a week. Felicitas, my wife, went to get her. Carmen couldn't speak any Spanish, had no good clothes. We taught her Spanish and sent her to adult school. Carmen is about 39 years old now and very successful. She studied to be a lawyer. She lives in Mazatlán, and she has her own business.

"I was born in the state of Oaxaca on September 28, 1951. I will be 63 this month. I was born in the pueblo of Tlaxiaco, where they speak the local dialect - Mixteco. When I came to the U.S. from Mexico, I brought a birth certificate that said September 28, 1951. However, I lost my birth certificate and I had to send for a new one. Someone made a mistake and put the wrong date on it. They put on the 24th. So that's the date I now use in the U.S. The true date is the 28th. Four days apart.

"I am named Carmen. My dad, who had never gone to school and could not read, heard the name 'Carmen'. He thought, 'All names that end with an 'A' are women's, and of course it doesn't end with an 'A,' so we will name the child Carmen.' That was it. I didn't change my name, or change the date I was born. There are people who do that, because they have problems in Mexico. Then they come here and change their name, or have problems here in the States and get renamed, but not me.

"My grandparents were born in the pueblo of Santiago Nuyoo. My paternal grandfather died very young; I saw him when he was dying. He had a disease similar to cancer and died. My grandmother brought him to our house in her arms. My maternal grandfather was, at that time, a landowner. He had land and cattle, but they had no money; they had property. They had goats, sheep, and chickens. Where they lived, there were mountain lions that ate the goats. So my grandfather had lots of dogs - the good kind, not those that sleep in, those that defend you. Because there was no electricity then, no medical help or medicine, no lamps. Dogs were the guardians.

"My parents were also born in Santiago Nuyoo. In the native language I speak it means 'moon face.' I had three sisters. The oldest died a month and a half ago - she was old and sick and died in Oaxaca, Mexico, where she lived. Another sister now lives in an *ejido*, (communal land ownership) in a place called Plan de San Luis. It is a place where the government hands out large amounts of land to the people who are called *ejidatarios* (co-op members); my third sister lives where my parents were born, in Santiago Nuyoo.

"Tlaziaco was a neighborhood, so to speak. It was spread apart. It was a community of only 4 houses. The homes were not right next to each other. If or when we could not finish the work in the fields, our neighbors came and helped us. And when they were late with their harvests, we would help them.

"As a young child I did not wear clothes. I am from a native race that did not wear clothes. No toys. We played with stones, flowers, frogs, snakes, cockroaches. Plants in the water (clean, not like here, where there is a lot of pollution). When I was five years old, I already worked. Our house was made of grass; from *sacate* leaves, banana leaves. My parents used the leaves to build our house. Ours was a *sacate* home. As it was made from banana leaves, when it rained, we got wet. During the rainy season we used to go live in caves. In the caves, water didn't enter; it was dry. We slept in the cave; the fire was lit, and my mom cooked and the goats we had slept next to us. My dad checked that there were no lizards, snakes, scorpions, mice or raccoons in the cave. It was cold, very cold. There was no bathroom. We did everything on the ground. I remember it all - it seems like yesterday. My mom and dad sowed corn and tomato, chili and beans. We ate that. We didn't go to the store, didn't buy food, nothing.

"We were hungry all the time, but there were plenty of fruits; if you wanted to eat a mango, you went and took it from the tree. To eat meat, my dad had a 22 rifle; he would hunt at night, killing rabbits and raccoons. He hunted and arrived home at 5:00 a.m. and prepared everything. I helped him - I brought water. He speared the game and put it in the fire. Delicious.

"Growing up was really difficult, because there was so little food. My mom gave me five tortillas for five days. She'd say, 'Eat a tortilla on

Monday, and you will get mangos, guavas, bananas to eat. And on Tuesday, another tortilla, and you'll get fruit and drink water.' There was never enough food, and no clothes. I used the same shirt for two years. It broke and my mom would patch it.

"All my parents did was work. When we were little, 5, 6, 7, 8 years old, they worked. My mom made tortillas on a stone. Because we were little, our job would be to put wood on the fire. We had a blower and used it to catch the fire. My dad would go to work, sowing cornfields, banana, and coffee, far away. He worked in the mountains, where there were no other people. He did not like to go too far. He went there to plant coffee. He would arrive home three or four days later. My dad was paid in cash. They paid five pesos for a whole day's work with a machete. Five pesos was a lot of money then. Only my dad worked; my mom took care of the goats, so that they were not eaten by coyotes. We went to school and my dad worked in the fields.

"Still, I saw my dad often. He took me to school. I was the only boy in the family. But I had no shoes. It hurt my feet, but there were no shoes. Only my dad had a pair. I was barefoot. I could not work, because I was too small, but I fetched water from rivers. I retrieved water with a *bule*. It is a gourd like plant that grows in our area of Mexico. We cut it and it has seeds. We let it rot inside, and then took out all the seeds. Like a small pumpkin.

"Saturday and Sunday, I helped my dad plant corn, collect bananas and oranges and go sell it to other people. One time, when I was about nine years old, I walked with him from Santiago Noyoo to Tlaxiaco - from 1:00 a.m. to 8:00 p.m. the same day. Walk and walk and walk with my dad. We carried fruit, bananas and ginger and sold it. My dad was carrying a sack of coffee and sold it and got money. We arrived home at 8:00 p.m., walking all day.

"There was no school close to where we lived, so we went to Santiago Noyoo. I had a tiny battery transistor radio and I listened to music on the way from my house to school. It was four hours each way. I went with my sisters. There was a shift from 8:00 a.m. to 1:00 p.m., and again from 3:00 to 6:00. We went to school all day, both shifts. Right now, the students enter at 8:00 or 9:00 in the morning, but at 3:00 or 4:00 they leave. We stayed at the school from Monday to Friday, because it was far away. We did not live at school. We lived at my grandmother's house. To get to school, we left at 4:00 or 5:00 a.m., when it was still dark and we had no lamps.

"My dad never sent us to school when we could already work in the field. Once I was of age, I helped him collect corn, fetch firewood, cared for the goats and got *chapulines* (they are small insect like grasshoppers that could be sold in to be eaten).

"When we were not in school or helping with chores, we played basketball. Our community bought some balls and gave us the balls to play with at recess. We also played on the swings, to and fro. At home, there was never anything - my dad never bought toys. The toys were rocks, frogs, and grasshoppers, cutting firewood, grabbing a stone and grating it over another one. My sister and I had races - we would run up the mountain, rolling downhill.

"I got to the sixth grade, but I was kicked out of school because I never passed it. I was 16, and should have been in high school, but did not pass. Because I had to walk very far, I hardly went to school. If you didn't do your homework, or didn't answer the question the teacher asked, or if you did not come early, or did not do your homework, the teacher used a ruler - you stretched your hands and the teacher hit you or they would pull your sideburns. Otherwise, they made you stand near the blackboard holding a brick.

"I liked grammar, writing and reading fast, but did not learn in school. I learned very little. The only one who spoke Spanish was the teacher; all the rest spoke indigenous languages. Most of the time, I did not understand what the teacher explained.

"I learned to write and I learned to speak Spanish outside of school. I also learned how to not have fear. I was in town with my dad, when some Americans arrived. My dad told me, 'These people are Americans; they do not speak Spanish, they speak English. They're American, do not go near them.' He was afraid. I don't know why. But they say that for the human being it's better to be afraid, because it's like a defense.

"Because there was no money, when I grew older I joined the Mexican Military. It was very hard, but it was voluntary. I told my mom I did not want to work in the field anymore, because there were so many dangerous animals and poisonous snakes. Once they bite you, bye. I told her I wanted to go into the army to earn money fast. Four months later, when I was 22 years old, I put on my uniform. I made some money, part of which I sent to my mom.

"The Military has a lot of discipline. They make you jump into the thorns, and push you into the water. You learn to climb up towering mountains. You had to jump on cacti. We did many push-ups and learned to walk across the rocks and the mountains. You had to cross a river with the water up to your chest. You couldn't remove your clothing. You had to run Tuesday and Thursday mornings. You had to learn how to jump over a table, from here to there. You had to run from here, jump and fall on the other side. If you fall with your heels, it hurts, but if you fall with the tip of the foot, it's okay.

"The basic instruction for the Mexican Military was four months. They cut your hair, teach you how to greet, teach you how to read books, teach you to disarm and to fire a weapon. After four months, you are the same as a veteran and can now perform a service. After that, you can advance - you can go up in grade and then they pay you more. I reached the rank of sergeant.

"After training, we went to catch bad people. Many would tell me, 'Kill him.' But inside my heart, I couldn't do that. It was not part of my nature. I did not know that, but in my heart I was not born to harm another person. So, the military sent others to kill, and they did it.

"In the Military, I was in Mazatlán and Sinaloa. I worked in the State of Chihuahua, and part of Sonora. I was working all the time and saw a lot of violence. We would go for six months to the mountains where there was drug trafficking. We had to destroy acres of marijuana and poppies. When there was no road, we had to go down with a rope from a helicopter. They lowered a rope and hung us way down, one by one, because the chopper couldn't land where there were only mountains.

"I remained in the army for 18 years. I made a lot of money in the military. I thought, 'If I resign, they will give me a lot of money and I'll make a deal.' Others told me, 'You have two years left until retirement. Wait two more years and you can retire and you are going to make money permanently.' But I didn't wait. I left on April 8, 1990, after 18 years - two years too early to get a pension.

"When I left the army, I stayed for two more years in Mexico. I moved from Tlaxiaco, where I was born, to the city of Oaxaca. In Oaxaca, I worked four months in construction earning good money. Because I was still relatively young, I was accepted to work on a construction site. I did what is called hard construction (it's different from the U.S.). You need to pick up 50 or 60 pounds on your own. Then I went to Mazatlán,

Chiapas, Durango then to La Paz. I did not travel for leisure - I went looking for work in all those places.

"I had wanted to create my own business in Oaxaca, but a friend asked me to come to the U.S. My friend brought me to the United States in 1993, when I was 42 years old. I came with him, alone. I was already married to Felicitas. I met her as a little girl in elementary school. My wife and I are of the Indian race. We got married when we were 27 and 30 years old, in 1982 in Plan de San Luis. We never got divorced. My wife taught me a lot - she taught me how to stop saying swear words, how to make cookies and how to sew with a sewing machine. But, to come to the United States, I left my wife in Tlaxiaco with my daughter Rocío, and my adopted daughter Carmen and came to the U.S. with my friend.

"My friend knew a coyote; he had used him before. He had been in the U.S. before and had left. We traveled by bus for 23 hours from Oaxaca to Mexico City. From there, another 18 hours to Tijuana, Mexico. That is where I crossed. I paid the coyote about $450. We crossed the border walking with the coyote and with about five other people. We walked through the desert. I was in great physical condition, because I had been in the army - so it was easy for me. It took, more or less, on average, five hours of walking, during the day. We left Tijuana at 3:00 a.m. We had a suitcase, a backpack with water, and good shoes. A change of clothes, nothing else. After we crossed the border, a car picked us up and took us to a house, where we bathed, changed clothes, and combed our hair. Then we boarded a plane at the airport in San Diego and flew to the airport in San Jose, California.

"For me it wasn't difficult, because I went through rougher times. I had been in the army for 18 years. I could walk all day without food, with only clean water. I could sleep standing up. I could walk all day while it rained. I could cross a river that could kill you. I could run 10 km with lots of gear, in the sand, at the beach. Uphill and downhill. On the grass and on the pavement. Heat. I was in great physical condition, so walking from Tijuana to the other side wasn't very difficult. With the training they gave us in the Army, everything I saw in Tijuana and during the crossing, I looked at without fear; I had already seen it all.

"Also, while I was in the Army I saw people being murdered, people being kidnapped. While we were crossing the border, we saw dead people and sick people. People crying, children. I had seen all that in Mexico. So, when I was crossing the border, I saw it as something I had experienced before.

"When I arrived in San Jose, California I knew for sure I had work, food, and clothing. I had a friend who lived in Mountain View, California and worked hard. He had come alone from Mexico - had left his wife and children and came here. He got me a job. I didn't struggle to get work, where to sleep, clothing or food. Everything was done. The first day, I arrived and I went to work. Working as a janitor.

"The person who brought me here to America gave me work, but he abused me, hit me, and left me lying there. Do you know San Tomas Expressway? In San Jose, California? He left me there and I did not know anything, - whether to go north or south. I knew nothing. I had worked twelve hours - all night and it was freezing. It was December. He left me lying there in the street. I have not forgotten - bleeding in the face. We had had an argument about a job that was done wrongly in the bathrooms. He had no education and was very big and strong and he hit me and left me. I do not consider him an enemy now; punishment will come on its own. Sometimes I run into him, he lives near here. 'Hi Pedro, how are you? How is your family? Nice to see you, congratulations, keep working.'

"My wife and daughter, Rocío, came to the U.S. in 1998, five years later. I had sent for them, because my wife had worked while I was in the U.S. and saved money. They came with a tourist visa, but overstayed. Then they had to go back, due to a family emergency and could not come back together. They were caught by immigration and separated at the border. But, they were able to reunite in Mexicali at a friend's house. Then I arranged for them to cross separately, but with the same coyote.

"But by then, I was lost in the drink ... I do not like to talk about that, because it does not sound good. I felt most alone in life when I had a drinking problem. Because it's bad. But it is better to live with problems, then to have nothing. From the problems you learn. One's life is like piano keys, there are black keys and white keys, that's life. The black keys are the enemies of us, diseases, debts, problems, and no job. The white keys are the future. But the two go together. The person who has no problems is a weak person.

"When my daughter, Rocío, first arrived with my wife, she was nine years old. I went to get them in Los Angeles. They crossed the border with a visa. They did not walk. They had a tourist visa. My family, my wife's family, my sister's family, no one had gone to college, no one had studied, nothing but the first grade, third grade, nothing more. My wife, Felicitas said, 'If we're going to have a daughter, she will have to study.' My wife and I were both day workers, but we sent our daughter, Rocío, to school.

"We had this dream of us arriving, going to a university, speaking English, and speaking other languages, and visiting other countries. Not having to speak the native language all the time, but learning something. We wanted to take advantage of the opportunity. But we did not know how it is here.

"Let's take an example... a person comes from Argentina. Arrives in the U.S. This is his house and that's his job. From home to work, from work to home, work, home. For 40 years, for 50 years ... knowing that it's the land of opportunity, and not taking advantage of it. That happens to me still. Most people live like that - it sounds harsh but it's true. They do not realize there is an opportunity in this country. There's a lot of money. We're still poor. I do not know how to start a business that you can grow.

"When I first arrived in the U.S., the first 5, 6, 7 years I was happy, but as it progressed I got older; I felt tired. One does not walk fast any more, we do not want to learn English, as well. There are obstacles, but it is not anyone's fault, it's my own fault. I can't blame Obama, the police, my daughter or my wife that I don't know English; it's my responsibility.

"I have a mentor, he lives in Sunnyvale. When I first came, I lost a lot of work, and he told me to come to see him. 'I will not give you money or a job - I'll give you an idea of how to do things. If you want to work, you will cut your nails, cut your hair, use clean clothes, walk fast and walk straight. Greet people. I'll teach you a greeting not to use. This greeting is called, 'dead fish'. It creates distrust, because I'm squeezing the hand. The proper greeting is like this: 'Hello, how are you?' And I corrected everything little by little. If I have a job and the boss leaves, I'd do the work as if he were watching me; I do not feel like, 'The boss is gone, now I can rest.' No, I am not like that.

"I am very reliable - if I have a job, I arrive 20 minutes early. I have been always like this, because the army disciplined me. If you do not arrive on time, you are out. Then I got used to always arriving on time. Do the job well. For you to get work, you have to change your attitude, speak well, say no curse words, cut your hair, wear clean clothes, and walk 25% faster than anyone else. Then they see your good attitude. A lazy person has a bad attitude, doesn't do things correctly, is late, does not bathe or mouths off.

"If the police grabbed me, I'd go willingly, if I'd made a mistake. But stealing, hurting someone or hitting someone, or using a weapon, or using a knife, no. I'll tell you, I will never do it. In this country, if you do things well, no one bothers you. When I worked as a janitor, all night, I was alone and traveled to Los Gatos, San Jose, South San Francisco, and Oakland. I came and worked one day here and a day there. I liked to return home driving on the streets, because all the traffic lights were green. But there always were policemen around. In 2009 I was stopped 14 times at night. I have been driving for about 10 years without a license. The police stopped me, because I was alone in the street. They flashed their lights and said, 'What are you doing at this hour?' 'Working.' 'Where do you work? And your license?' 'I work over there, clean an office and I don't have a license ...' 'Okay, go.' And they let me leave. One day my car turned off and I was stranded in front of the light, red, green, red, green, and the car didn't work. The police came and helped me. They helped me push the car off the street. They never took my car. I have a few tickets for not stopping at a stop sign, turning outside the time, or because of a busted taillight, but not for any serious violations. If the police stop me, I say, 'Sir, here's my license. I did not stop because I did not see it.' Without using profanity. I do not get a ticket. I like it when there are lots of police, because it is their job.

*****

"I am now 63 and my sister from Oaxaca is 64. My sister that died was 65 and my youngest sister is 55. I only speak with the one that lives in San Luis Plan de Oaxaca. She lives there, and she learned to speak a little Spanish, but she speaks the indigenous language beautifully. When I talk to her, it gives me a good laugh, because she has a very nice tone. I talk to her in the indigenous language only. She wants me to come back to Mexico, to her home and eat corn tortillas. I want to go.

"My father died five years ago. My mom died in 1978. My dad was left alone and remarried. He had another son, my half-brother. He came here to the States and settled in Virginia. When my dad died my stepbrother returned to Plan de San Luis, because my dad left him 26 acres to raise cattle. There was no one to take care of the land, so he left the States. I am also his son and I have a legitimate right to the land, too. I can be the owner of these properties, but I have a different idea. It's not something I want. My stepbrother is now caring for the land. It's a lot of ground. It has water, springs and cedar trees.

"I heard about the Day Worker Center from my daughter, Rocío. Since she was a little girl, she liked accessing information and surfing the internet. I had been laid off of work and I was going to return to Mexico, but Felicitas, my wife, told me not to go. We were paying $450 in rent, but my wife told me, 'You have to recycle.' I collected lots of bottles and cans and went to San Jose, Sunnyvale, Mountain View, East Palo Alto, and Menlo Park on my bike and got money from recycling. Then my daughter found the web page for the Day Worker Center in Mt. View. And I came to the Center and have stayed here as a day worker for about six years. At the Center, we get jobs and also have classes. People come and talk about immigration reform. We also get people talking about how to grow a business, how to make money, how to put a business together. People talk about our health care. They give us ideas.

"While I am at the Center, I want to learn gardening and plumbing, but learn from the beginning. Right now, I can't get a job in a company because of my age. But if you get there when you're young, they'll give you a job. As I mentioned, my first job was as a janitor with my friend Pedro. Then I went to a company called Ramirez Janitorial. I didn't like that job, because you do not learn anything, it was very simple. It made no sense. I just cleaned here, dusted and left. But electrical work, plumbing, gardening, and architecture are interesting areas. Sometimes I work as a gardener in the houses around the Center. I like working on the land. I like plants – I was born among them.

"Near the Day Worker Center, there is a lady's place I go to for two or three hours, but she pays me more than $15 an hour, because I arrange her plants pretty well. Whenever I worked there, I would be careful not to step on anything, I'd leave everything spotless, and if there was more, I'd clean more. I'd do it in less time, and when the lady comes out, she looks up and says, 'Hey, you've arranged my garden beautifully.' When I work for this lady, instead of going to work, 2, 3, 5, 8 hours - I go for 2 or 3 hours and she pays me $100. And I do not ask her when she'll pay, or at what time I have to leave. I arrive and do a good job. She likes it.

"One day, through the Day Worker Center, I went to work for a man who had a big garden. He said, 'Get off the machine and go buy grass,' with a nasty tone. 'Then what do I do?' 'Pick up the trash, and we'll go.' He spoke to me like that. You should not talk to a person in that way. If you are working for me, I'm not going to talk to you like that. I'd say, 'Come, let's do this job, let's mow the lawn, and once we finish, you and I are going to take the tools up, and we're done.' Better communication needs to be used. You shouldn't say, 'You do' and 'I won't do it.' The man brought me back to the Day Worker Center. He said, 'Did you like it or not?' but loudly. And I do not use that tone. I told him, 'The reason you have not grown your business is because you have not changed your attitude.' I told him, 'Your business has not grown, you just do the work, physically, all you do is the work. Because you can't communicate with people, you do not know how to treat people.' Serving the people is very different. You should say, 'Come, and you and I will do it together.' You can't say to people, 'Do it, and fast.' I gave him ideas; I didn't scold him. He answered me with swear words, but I didn't scold him.

"I want to learn carpentry and plumbing. I want someone to say, 'Here is a carpentry shop. There's a man who will teach you.' If I had a place like that, I would go. One Sunday, I worked with an architect. I know nothing about how to hold a tool and put in a nail; I don't know how to cut wood. But the man taught me with a lot of patience. The man said, 'Carmen, handle it like this, put the weight of your body behind it, place the nail, put this here and use this tool.' He taught me. I liked it. He was not one of those people who say, 'Move away, I'll do it because you do not know how to.' He told me, 'Pick it up like this, use your body weight as well, mark it with your pencil and use this saw and cut it.' I would like to find a place to learn, not for the money, but to learn.

"The hardest part of my life is that I do not know English and have no close friends - only friends that I drink with. I have some friends from the Day Worker Center. How do you feel when you talk with someone like a friend, with a good attitude? It feels nice. Sometimes, when I talk to the people I know at the Day Worker Center, I tell them a little about my story. I talked to my friend a bit about where I came from. I came here and did not speak Spanish well, and did not understand anything - let alone English. I said that I was very poor, not poor in ideas, poor in the sense that I'm seeing that you're eating, food, breakfast, lunch and dinner and I have nothing. As a child there were people who ate good food and I watched. I was hungry but my dad taught me to never steal.

"Not everyone in my family is like me. I have nothing. Others in my family are architects, doctors. They have properties and they have homes. Not the same life that I have. They have families who are in the States or in Mexico; others are in the army. But they are good, not like the life I had. Felicitas and I were the ones that were out of medicine, food, clothing, education and money to study.

"Now I live in an apartment with my wife and daughter, Rocío, who is 26 years old. We live near the Day Worker Center in a one-bedroom apartment. The reason I rent a one-bedroom apartment is that my daughter is old enough - she needs to have privacy. She said to us, 'You can sleep in the living room.' My wife and I live in the living room and sleep on the couch. We get up to cook in the kitchen. And then we do the cleaning twice a week. My daughter put her office in her room. She's in there and we are here. Everyone has their own bookcase. Rocío has a huge bookcase and I have a bookcase. Felicitas, my wife, has one too.

"The monthly expenses are difficult. Rent is $1,630. But we share it. Our apartment complex is not a place where Latinos typically live. It's in an area where students live, places where Google engineers live. Here, they do not make noise. We pay the rent first. We can run out of food, but rent comes first. I was taught to be responsible with the rent. It is paid on the 25th or 28th of each month. We share the cost of rent. I give the money to my daughter. She puts the money in her account and the rental company automatically removes it from there.

"I want my daughter to become an independent entrepreneur, for her not to work long; I want her to become a free person by the time she is 30 or 35, with spare time (just like some other people), and money and for her to travel around the world, for her not to need to return to work. I don't know if she has a boyfriend. I do not ask. I always say, 'You have to have a family, you cannot be alone. Pretend you are like a flower that will wither on the tree, sad and lonely. You have to find a partner and start a family. Have one or two children and educate your children. Not how I started.'

"I hope she can raise a family, and not rely on a boss that pays you very little money. It's not bad to work, but it's bad to get permanent work, with no money and paying rent. It is better to build a home. People that make their money work for them are free. Success is not having much money, but having style.

"I eventually want to return to Mexico. I am lonely here – I have no true friends. The other day, when I was watching television, I saw that Mexico is not like when I left. The town where I grew up now has many roads, TV, phone, and the internet. There are good homes. There are no *sacate* houses, nothing like that. But it is very polluted. When I was there as a child, the water was clean, there were no cars ... clean. But not now.

"I think, 'Why didn't I study when I was young?' It's not my dad's fault. It is not because there was no money. It is because of me. Even though I am as old as I am right now, I would like to learn. I'm willing to work for no money, but I want to learn, because what you learn is valuable. What helped me was when I switched to the Christian life. I stopped swearing, I stopped drinking. I had no friends. I had friends, but drinking ones. Then I started to write notes and repeated them and practiced with another person. 'If you dress well, that does not count; what counts is the inside, the heart. When you change, you can change the world.'

"To lead a good life is to do good to someone else, help someone else, and give to those that have no food, because money is not everything. There are many people who have a lot of money, but do not have the idea of sharing. But a person who has money and shares, will always live in a quiet place. They will live happily, and give thanks to God for each new day. When you wake up in the morning, give thanks.

"In life there are two paths, there are good ways and bad ways. But we need both. There is a lady who comes to the center, called Lourdes. I ask, 'How are your children?' 'They are very rebellious,' she says. I say, 'No. You are the mirror of your kids, there are no bad kids, and those kids are bad because you raised them. Stand at your bathroom mirror and look at yourself. You are the mirror of your children. A person who has no problems is a weak person.' And, I said, 'Do not give your children many toys, because they will grow weak. Give gifts as they respond, as they grow. If you are a good student, I'll give you a gift. If you are a good engineer, I'll give you a hug, I'll give you my love, give love.'

"To be remembered, you have to do great things. I do not think I'll get a statue or a monument. No. Did you know your grandfather? Your great-grandfather? No, because they didn't do great things, so we do not know them. If they had done big things for future generations, we would be seeing them in a photo and hearing their story. For example, this one was an engineer. This one left an inheritance to his grandchildren; this one was a writer, he left many books. As they did nothing, we do not know them.

"I regret coming here to the United States. For me, where I came from, Plan de San Luis, is a beautiful place. There's no road, but there is a river and the boys who studied with me in primary school made their houses on the banks of the river, and they are bankers or have made a lot of money through farming. The river is like a road between the state of Veracruz and Oaxaca. Everything that's produced on one side of the river is sold on the river. All the products that are produced here; they sell it on the river and they've made a lot of money as entrepreneurs. I want to return to Plan de San Luis.

"I told my sister who lives in Plan de San Luis that I'm going to build a house on a mountain where she lives. I'm going to make a house there, because she has a spring. It's like a hole and the water is very clean water. And on this land, I'll get seed, have cattle, have two dogs, big sheep dogs and live there and have a car and be close to children."

Chapter 8 (Continued)

Rocío's Story

"I came to the U.S. when I was nine years old with my parents, Carmen and Felicitas. I have no memories of Mexico. I probably do, but I don't think about Mexico that much. My first memory of the U.S. – what surprised me the most – was the roads – they were so long. Because after we crossed the border, we drove from Los Angeles to the San Francisco Bay Area. The first time I came was with a visa that eventually expired. We were here for a year or two. Then, we decided to go back to Mexico to try and figure out a way to come into the States legally – but it didn't work. We could not get a return visa, so my parents paid a coyote and we came over the border again. I remember it was very difficult to adjust to the culture and learn the language. Very, very difficult."

Rocío is a petite young woman with long dark brown hair, tan skin and a bright smile. She speaks eloquently and intelligently about growing up as an undocumented person and attending school in the Bay Area. Rocío's father describes her as "a very restless person. A person who wants to invent something and would make millions of attempts to achieve it."

When she arrived in 1998, she lived in East Palo Alto and attended public school. Her teacher in public school thought she excelled beyond other students, and contacted her parents to recommend that she apply to Eastside College Preparatory, a middle school and high school in East Palo Alto, CA, a lower income area located halfway between San Francisco and San Jose, CA., within several miles of Stanford University. The school was started by a Stanford graduate as an independent, tuition-free school for students from 6th through 12th grades who have shown promise of becoming the first in their families to attend college. At this time, over 60% of the student body is Latino. The school is sponsored by local real estate developers, venture capitalists and other wealthy individuals.

"I was very lucky in that I actually went to private school. That was my first opportunity. During the time I was at Eastside, I had a mentor - Chris. This is a person I have stayed in touch with, even since I graduated. Having a mentor like her was the beginning of everything for me. She was really more than just a mentor and friend. She was an advocate – like a parent. With her guidance, I started traveling while I was in middle school. With her help, I went to D.C., I went to Atlanta, and I went to all these conferences on journalism and other subjects. And I remember, Chris always prepared me – she took care of my flights – not financially, but she gave me guidance – what to expect – things you would normally, as a kid, get from your parents. Many parents have been through it–for example, they know when you need to apply for college so you do not miss the deadline. My parents and most immigrants did not have that kind of experience to impart to their children.

"I worked hard and graduated Eastside Prep with a 4.0 GPA. I had an interest in journalism and theater. I was accepted into several very good universities. I received a scholarship from the Rotary Club of Menlo Park and attended Columbia University in New York City.

"College was difficult. I became depressed, but I could not tell my parents. My parents would not understand the pressures I was going through. I was no longer the A student and I was at the bottom. My mentor, Chris, from Eastside Prep, took me by the hand and helped me through the situation. I feel better now.

"My mentor was like a parent and opened up her whole network to me. Her husband happened to be a very well-known executive back in the day. And, because his wife had faith in me, he also opened his network to me. Especially when I was applying for jobs – wow, that makes a difference. I remember, I was applying to Deloitte. I had submitted my resume and her husband made this call to this acquaintance or friend that he had in Deloitte, and the following day there was a follow-up call and the interview happened right away. The same thing happened with McKinsey. I have always realized that it makes an incredible difference in your career, your life, to have these kinds of advocates help open doors.

"The other part is that the mentoring also helped my social life. There were things that I didn't know going into Columbia – like the Homecoming – because I never had that. I went to a really tiny school. We didn't even have a prom. It was invaluable, having someone who exposed me to dining out and country clubs. I could be at the same level as the other students at Columbia.

"While I was at Columbia, I was making zero money. Every summer, it was a struggle to find an internship, because of my immigration status. Even if I could work for free, for example, in the United Nations in N.Y., I could not afford to rent an apartment in NYC for the summer. So I had to come back here to the Bay Area. I remember that during that time, in the summer, my parents were sharing a two-bedroom apartment with another family. They only had one room. I remember that summer made a big difference for me, because while I was living in the room with my parents, I could actually save up the money I made from my internship in the place I worked. I could spend that money during the school year. That was better than living in N.Y. during the summer, and spending for food and all that. And it helps, because I got the internship experience – it is on the resume – and on the other hand, I had money for the year. That's what was really important.

"I graduated from Columbia University with a degree in economics in 2011. Because of my illegal status, I could not go into investment banking, which is what I wanted to do. So I had to be creative about what to do. I started doing marketing for a real estate company here in Silicon Valley - a company in Palo Alto. I didn't know this at the time, but I remember, what drew me into marketing wasn't necessarily the branding, or the things in design, or putting the catalogues together, the pamphlets, but it was the database. The company had a huge database with many real estate contacts. Basically, we would bombard people with email. For me, that was very annoying, because I thought, wait a minute, why are you sending the same email to all these different people. They have different needs. One is looking for a condo and one is looking for a house. Someone is looking under one million dollars and someone is looking for something more expensive. And it bothered me. So I organized all their data.

"Later on, I could legally work under a program called DACA (Deferred Action for Early Childhood Arrivals). This program started in 2012. People like me – children of undocumented workers - can get two years of work authorization and they can renew it every two years until they are 30 or unless the government decides to end it. It is not a law, it is not an executive order, but it is just a temporary relief program – a memorandum authored by the Obama administration and implemented by the Department of Homeland Security. It is basically a grant of deferred removal action and does not confer lawful immigration status or provide a path for citizenship. It can end when the President leaves office or at any time.

"When I got my DACA permit, I could apply for any job. I actually decided to go into technology. I stayed in marketing and I started doing business cases for different marketing programs at Cisco Systems. I wasn't happy with it and then finally, by serendipity, I was thrown into a stretch assignment. I always knew that I liked to understand people, understand behavior. And this was the perfect opportunity, because it allowed me to do design for the first time. That's how I started discovering that I really loved to understand behavior. And then, through experiences I had at work, I began to realize that there was actually something called user experience. And I can do this on a full time basis. I am thinking about changing to that. Within or outside of Cisco – we'll see.

"I would like to remain in design - design experiences for products and services. But the thing that drives me, especially now, is that I finally found what makes me passionate. It is basically that, in design, you are conveying an idea. A simple idea. And that idea can potentially change people's lives. But in order to get to that idea, you need to be able to communicate so well – so proficiently. I think that people like Steve Jobs were able to do this so well. Of course he would curse and do all these things, but ... to be able to have that level of simplicity and convey it through your design, that's beauty.

"My perspective is that there is actually something interesting that is happening in Silicon Valley. There are people like my parents who came here in the 1990s and work here in janitorial or service types of jobs. And immigrants like my parents bring their kids as well. Then the kids grow up here and they become Americanized. Later on, some of these children go on to college and then they are able to become a guide for their parents.

"Here in Silicon Valley, immigrant parents are relying more on their kids. Especially in this particular area, because this area is very expensive. The younger people that are moving here for technology jobs are pushing up the house prices - and the rents. For example, I was actually in East Palo Alto this week and went to drop my mom off and I was just looking at East Palo Alto. I had not been there for 4 years, since 2010. I kept seeing along the street, houses for sale. I was actually curious to see how much the price was. Surprisingly, the house that I was looking at was half a million dollars –this is in a low-income part of the Bay Area. The demographics will definitely change because of these price increases. The population will probably become more Asian and less Latinos and African Americans.

"So what happens is that people like my father, who is a day worker and probably makes $200 to $400 per week - that honestly doesn't mean anything, but it still helps them a lot. Then, you find the next generation is carrying on or supporting the family, as well. Because the lifestyle, here in Silicon Valley, has definitely gone up and it will continue to increase over time as more people are coming in. And then, you find that more immigrant families are moving south to Sunnyvale, San Jose, and Gilroy. But East Palo Alto is the only place that has rent control in the Valley. So there are really not many places that people like my parents – day workers – can go. It is going to be a challenge, because they are serving the community here in Silicon Valley, in Palo Alto, Los Altos, Los Altos, Hills, and Mt. View. There is going to be a commute. The commute will take longer. And there have to be trade-offs, because some of these families have kids. Do I go to the Day Worker Center or drop off my kid at school that now happens to be 40 minutes south of here and there is traffic in the morning? That is definitely a trend. It is already happening and we will continue to see it intensify over the next few years.

"So the challenge is, we need to understand these families and understand where they are coming from and what they can contribute. Actually, here is the beauty. And I do not think many people see it yet. There are families like my parents that are undocumented and they are immigrants and they are service people, but they brought a child with them. And that child somehow happened to go to school and then to college. And some children of immigrants are working in technology and other industries. Well, as more families have the same success, they are bringing their kids and they may, at some time, be able to contribute to the business world. Which right now, I have to say, is only one perspective.

"I am a designer. And when we think about design, especially in the company where I work, the perspective is to think about the typical person; to understand his wants and needs. The typical person is a Mike or a Rachel, someone who is the typical American. But the reality is the demographics are changing. And we need people like myself or children from these immigrants, who can reflect that this technology is not only going to be used by Caucasians, but is also going to be used by Latinos and African Americans.

"Someone who happens to live in a more affluent community and owns a house needs someone to realize how important his support is for day workers. He needs to see that someone is coming to do his gardening at $12 per hour, but that person may have a child and they are putting him through school or just that they are paying rent. And it makes a big difference that you are giving them that money.

"I remember at one time, my dad was working at the Day Worker Center and I do not remember what my mom was doing. But I remember him doing the Day Worker jobs, plus he was also doing recycling. And he did not even have a car, so he was using his bike to carry big bags of recycled goods. In 2007-2011 - that was in the middle of the financial crisis. But rent was about still $1000 per month – it was still quite a lot for them. Now a one bedroom is more expensive - around $1800. We live in a one-bedroom place now and my parents sleep in the living room. It is expensive – it is almost $1900 for our one bedroom. I help my parents with the rent, of course.

"I just received my new DACA card, so that will be valid until 2016. That gives me another year. My parents will be fine here in California. What worries me most is how the area is changing so fast. It is kind of turning against them; not against them like throwing them out; just that rents are increasing and it is hard to find service jobs. So I actually have been considering moving. I don't know yet. I will probably be moving at some point in my life. The challenge is taking my parents with me. I've been to the East coast, I've been all over and I have not found a place like the San Francisco Bay Area. In the sense that people here are very generous, and they are actually willing to help you if you tell them what you need. But it is still so hard.

"It will be up to the next generation to support and help out. Just like I am doing right now. That's the other thing this area – we have done a great job bringing in profits and making products that have changed people's lives. The next level is we need to educate young kids in less advantaged neighborhoods, like East Palo Alto and East Menlo Park (lower income areas) that you do not have to do what your parents did – which is get a job and stay with a company 20 years. We need to show them the alternatives.

"Marc Zuckerberg, the founder of Facebook, was teaching an Entrepreneur101 class in one of the middle schools in East Menlo Park. And when he went there, he asked the kids in the class what were their dreams and aspirations. One of them raised his hand and said 'I really can't do this, because I am undocumented.' And that's when it hit him – this is something that worries this community. Zuckerberg's non-profit organization is called 'FWD.us' and is trying to bring awareness to immigration reform. However, even this organization is about immigration reform in the context of we need more HV1 Visas for the technology community, not necessarily the whole comprehensive immigration reform.

"Unfortunately, it is going to take time. For example, even at Cisco Systems, I am one of the few Latinas in the company directory. Looking at the marketing organization – which is around 1500 people, I am one of the only Latinas, except for the assistants or the janitors. It is shocking. I was looking at Fortune 500 companies and I would have thought that by now they would have taken advantage of the diversity card. Unfortunately, the level of qualification is part of it. Also, they don't take risks when they hire people - especially because they have to answer back to shareholders. But I think, if you can get this idea to kids – to take risks, it can make a big difference. For example, they can begin their own start-up; if you do have an idea, you need to go for it. But the problem is that immigrant parents don't have much knowledge about possibilities, because all they have known all their lives is that you do this and then you get paid and that is how you pay the rent. But there has to be some sort of way to show them that there are alternative paths to the American dream.

"I was reading this book by Christian Rudder; he is one of the co-founders of OkCupid – a free online dating service. His whole book is about all the data they have accumulated on his web sites. When I was reading through that book, I compared myself to what's expected of a Latina. I do not fit there. I probably fit more on a white spectrum. That's why, when I think of my mentor, Chris, I realize she helped me get into that spectrum. Not 'get' – she exposed me to it, so I could be better prepared, and actually gain advantage.

"I would like to become a citizen, but I am not sure that will happen anytime soon. I do not think the President will do anything–he is too nice. He is not willing to take risks. We'll see.

"The company I work for cannot do anything for me – there is really no way. I know it sounds really depressing, but there is really no way. I was talking to a friend a while back and he asked me why don't I get an HV1 visa. Or why don't you do 'x..y..z?' I was trying to explain to him that there is no way. We broke the law. We came here illegally. And if we were to go back, we would face a ten-year ban and we could not come back into the States. Anyone who is here illegally – even if you came with a visa and overstayed that visa. You broke the law. So you go back and you face a ten-year ban. I am not really into politics, but I can't help saying this: The system is just not working anymore for the 21st century. They really need to revamp it. Even while I was waiting for my DACA worker authorization to come in, it took a while, and I was thinking to myself, why does this take so long? Homeland Security runs the DACA program. The company I work for does not do anything to help me. They just know that I have this temporary work permit. They don't care. They do check status and I have a social security number. And I pay taxes As an outsider looking in or an insider looking out, the system just does not work anymore. While I was preparing the paperwork for DACA, I was thinking to myself, it is kind of like the DMV. It is painful, but you have to go through it. And unfortunately there is no competition, so you really can't innovate. I was thinking to myself, Oh God, this is sort of the same. I think to myself why is it so hard? Because if you just follow the rules, nothing gets done.

Chris

"I was a volunteer at Eastside Preparatory School in East Palo Alto. I know that Rocío had heard about Eastside while she was in primary school and very much wanted to go there. Eastside was well known in the public schools in East Palo Alto. It is the dream school of many Hispanic families.

"Rocío is a person who seeks out what she needs. It is the most amazing thing. In fact, if I were writing a story about her, I would say it is central to the story - that she makes her life happen. And she finds the people in her life that will make it happen. She is very proactive. And, so, I think that once she and her teacher talked about the possibility of Eastside, she said, 'I really want to go there.'

"Initially, I wasn't even working with her group. The way it is organized at Eastside is that, if you were volunteering there, you would get seven children to yourself and you would teach them their entire English program - literature, parts of speech, and vocabulary. The curriculum is very rigid so that everyone was delivered exactly the same program. So I was working with seven other seventh graders. Suddenly Rocío came to me and said, 'Would you help me? I am writing a book.' And her English was not what it is today. She said, 'I need to practice the English language, so I am writing a science fiction story.' She was on page three hundred and something. She asked, 'Would you edit it for me?' That's a lot of work to do, so I told her that I would just help her on the part of the book she was working on right then. 'We'll just work together on that,' and so we did that after class. She got transferred into my group. There were suddenly openings; two students moved from my group and I may have said, send Rocío to my group, since we are already talking and working together. As soon as she got there, we sort of took off working, on the side, as well as doing all the work in class.

"I only worked with her one year - in seventh grade. She was the star pupil. She just achieved at everything. I worked there another few years and, as she went up the grade levels, she would come to me and talk to me about what was going on. Our interaction after the first year was as friends. She was a sponge. She was the class leader. She was very serious about it and not particularly social. She was kind of a loner.

"This little girl, who was walking home to a house you or I would not want to live in, in East Palo Alto, living with 17 people. They shared the house in order to pay the rent. There were no other children in the home.

"She was already relating to her teachers more at Eastside than to her parents. And then you have two people at home who are very, very simple people. Her mother may not have gone to school at all and her father may have gotten up to the sixth grade. That is not a very stimulating situation at home. Everything had to come from within Rocío. And she would walk home from school on winter nights, down by the Dumbarton Bridge. She would never complain about it. She was a very determined little girl. Determination is key to understanding her.

"So after that first year, and as I said, she was the shining star, it became clear to me that she was going places. We just kept talking the other years I worked there. One of the things she wanted to do was to take extracurricular activities that would help her with her English. So she would challenge herself by joining the journalism team to write more. She would challenge herself to take leadership classes, photography, or whatever excited her. And this is, of course, a theme for her throughout high school and college. She over does; she picks the hardest curriculum you can have. She would take a regular load and three extra classes, because she was so excited to learn. So, we just became friends. I helped her understand 'first world life' in the Bay Area – that was part of our relationship. She had never even seen the ocean!

"We still talk, because we are friends. It was ongoing that we talked about life and the opportunities that would be available to her with an education. And I always stressed that she was on the right track. She talked about social things with me, but it was mainly that she did not feel truly a part of things. She had no interest in boys at that age.

"We talked about a whole host of things that she did not have the opportunity to talk to her mother or father about. She came to our home while she was in high school and that made a big impression on her. And, I used to take her to her home sometimes after school, and it was a scary situation. She certainly was one of the top graduates in her class. I saw her routinely through high school, but, once she went to Columbia, she would call me and we just kept the connection going. She knew I was there for her.

"Columbia was her number one choice. She got a free ride at Columbia. A total free ride. Her balance was zero every semester. It was extraordinary – food, housing. I think she had only to pay for books. All her classes, everything, was paid for. All the way through for four years. So, my husband and I would give her a little spending money. We also talked to her about budgeting – the same things we did with our children. I had a lot of very serious talks with her about budgeting – I am giving you this amount of money for spending money – and I definitely want you to see a play in New York City every semester She was so serious, she would just work, work, work.

"She was extremely stressed at Columbia. She refused to go to a counselor, which was a bone of contention between us. I really wanted her to reach out at the college for help. She did not feel comfortable with a counselor – it was not in her culture to do that. And her parents had no idea what to say and do to help her. Her parents loved her very much – she comes from a very loving couple. For a while she was more critical of her parents, I think, because of their limitations in education and experience. But, I think she is very appreciative of her parents and their love – she has really matured.

"At some point I thought she would quit college due to the stress. But I said, 'That is not an acceptable option. You have to stay there.' Not harshly. For her, it was lonely and miserable. Columbia is tough. She couldn't have picked a tougher school. She knew it was an elite school and that made her very happy.

"We also discussed planning. Figuring out what her week looked like. How much could she take on and still manage to do well. Those were long talks about making a plan. She wasn't seeing out far enough. She was just so excited about all the different classes offered. She would dabble in things. It was free to her. She took Chinese. She took dance, which has always been a real release for her. She has consistently gone back to it over the many years. It has been good for her social life. But there are huge gaps still in her being able to navigate through this culture.

"Her parents, Carmen and Felicitas, have been to my home. We had a party for Rocío when she graduated college. It was very small, with her parents and the adults in the community that have helped her and a couple of friends. Her parents were not able to communicate with me. It was an extremely moving day, because we had a formal party for her and she said that she had nothing to give us back – for all of us who had helped her. So she danced for us. It was a modern, interpretive dance, set to music that she had choreographed. It was unusual to have someone do that for you, but that is what she was able to give to us. It was beautiful and people were extremely moved.

"Her parents are beyond polite. When I would drop her off at home, they would always say, 'Thank you.' Her father, especially, is emotional. He adores her. Her mother is more reserved. Rocío pointed out that her parents have had no privacy in their relationship until she got them an apartment two years ago. It was the first time her mother has had a roof over her head that is hers. It was an emotional time for her parents – they were beyond grateful to have their privacy. Her mom and dad told her they felt like they were just starting their marriage. Before that, they had either lived apart (when Carmen was in the Mexican Army) or in a house with several other people. The three of them lived in a single bedroom. They had a little hot plate, and they could use the kitchen if they wanted to. She had to live in a room with her parents.

"After graduating Columbia, Rocío was more discouraged than ever. She did not have good job prospects after her unbelievably hard work over many, many years from the time she was twelve. This is a girl who looked on line and found a way to get into Columbia. She was on line constantly looking at all her possibilities. She was very proactive. And then all the work it took in high school and then all the work it took in college. And then she came out and could not get a job, because of her undocumented status. How unbelievably discouraging that was.

"She finally got a job at a real estate agency in Palo Alto. But we were having a long lunch and she told me she had to get out of there. 'I have changed their whole business plan and done everything I can do. I want to be in corporate America so badly.'

"I told Rocío that there was one person she ought to talk to – a friend of mine. Rocío told me she knew her, because she had house sat for her for two or three weeks one summer. I had recommended Rocío to her. This woman was one of the head people at Cisco Systems. I called my friend and asked if she would be willing to meet for coffee with Rocío and told her the situation. I told her she was undocumented. But Cisco was in the process of hiring 200 new young employees and this woman was in charge. I gave her Rocío's number and gave Rocío her number and they met for coffee. She got her an interview at the Company and told the people to get her a job. And she got a job.

"That was all happening while Obama was initiating the DACA program. Cisco was a little nervous and wanted to get the paperwork done. Rocío could not believe it. She got a great salary, she got DACA and she got a driver's license; she bought a car, she got her parents an apartment. It was like a fairy tale.

"Rocío is impatient already at Cisco. I have told her not to even think about making a change for two years. I do not care how bored you are – that paycheck is coming in every month. They like you, they have given you a raise. She has health care for the first time. But she is isolated, again. She may feel isolated, because Cisco is an aging company – it is not a young, dynamic company. And she really was bored there. But I do not think it is a good idea for her to start her own business. She has thought about working for a smaller company, where she would have a little more influence. She has spoken up to her bosses and gotten a few people to state what the problems are in the company. She is an outspoken person.

"I do not think it would be a bad idea if Rocío had to leave the States - for a corporate job - a sophisticated job - somewhere in the corporate world. I've asked, 'What's so terrible?' And Rocío answered, 'My parents.' If her dad wants to go back to Mexico, it could be a blessing in disguise. Her father is idealizing a return to Mexico. I do think he should be very careful about his influence over Rocío. Even if she went back to Mexico, she would get a good corporate job in Mexico City. She is an extremely educated person. And there are a lot of professionals in Mexico. So, she could survive that, and in ten years, it sounds like a million years to her, but if she left at thirty and came back at forty, she would probably marry down there; she would be in her own culture.

"I think she is working to feel part of this culture and to understand it. It will take a lifetime, because she was so excluded from it for so long. So much of your culture comes from your parents, we help our children. Our children have their parents as models. There are so many subtleties about being an immigrant.

"Rocío's social life has really evolved over the last year and a half. I think it is unfortunate that her entry into the U.S. may be through marriage. It colors dating. And she is very inexperienced in the dating world. She did not do any dating until her senior year in college.

"When we see each other, I will ask her, 'What do you think about everything?' I mainly listen. I give her advice where I can. I do think Rocío will come out on her feet. She will find a way. She is not brilliant, but she is just the most hardworking person you have ever met in your life.

"I think her biggest challenge is comfort in communication. She was not communicating well with people until she was at Eastside. So she is way behind. I would just say, Rocío is 'tough' to talk to – it does not flow. Part of this is just her personality – she is an introvert. Social things do not come easily. She works at them like she works at everything else.

"The future is very, very uncertain. She has DACA but only for 4 more years. Congress better do something about immigration. These are the 'dreamers', these are the kids, and they have no control over it."

Rocío

"The lives of the Latinos are not part of the lives of most people, and we have to make it part of our lives. It will come. We are seeing more couples marrying people from different cultures. For example, I probably date more Caucasian men and over time I will probably end up marrying one. People will become aware, because my kids will be hanging out in an upper middle class neighborhood. I can stay here if I marry someone who is a citizen, but I have not found that person.

"Now I need to be more aware of it. I have the pressure because in these next two years I need for my career to take off and bring more awareness to this somehow. And on the other side, I have the pressure to take dating more seriously. I am 26. The people that you socialize with may not necessarily know about the situation. The reason is because we are all so very disconnected. Over time, we are somehow going to start drawing in and then you will see more interracial marriage and, of course, more connection, I think that is when the government will finally do something. But it will take time."

Carmen

"I worry about my second daughter. The adopted girl we have in Mexico, she has her business already. My main concern is with Rocío, She will not last long working for someone else - she needs her own business. Whatever you want, I say to Rocío. I am on my way out, but do not worry a lot. I live with what we know today. Yesterday is past. You are tomorrow."

Epilogue

We are a nation of immigrants. Our parents, or grandparents or even more distant ancestors, came to this country, carrying with them memories of their past lives, as well as their own personal hopes, not knowing what the future held for them. Perhaps, they have shared their stories with you.

The next time you hear a friend, or relative or neighbor say, "I think all the undocumented workers should be sent back," consider asking, "Have you spoken to your gardener? Have you spoken to your housekeeper? Have you asked them if they are here legally or are undocumented? Have you asked them why they left their native countries? Most importantly, have you asked them about their children, their aspirations and their dreams?"

Discussion Questions

1. Salvador came to the U.S. with only the clothes he wore to cross the border. How did you feel when he cried because he did not have enough money to buy a shirt? How did you feel when he slapped his wife? Did this change your impression of him in any way? Do you think he will become a citizen?

2. Ernesto worked in Peru and Japan before coming to the U.S. What do you think of his attitude towards other workers? Towards the Japanese? The Mexicans? The Jews? Do you think he will get married to an American citizen and how do you feel about that?

3. In Lucia's story, was she wrong to rent out her sofa? How did you feel about the situation with their son's abuser? Lucia reported the abuse. Do you believe that other undocumented victims of abuse may hesitate to report crimes against themselves? Why?

4. Rubin came to the U.S. to be with his family. Why do you think he is unhappy here? Do you think his support of his unmarried son and his girlfriend and grandchild perpetuates a culture of unmarried parents?

5. Aurora sustained a serious injury while working in the U.S. and received a small settlement. Should that change her immigration status in the U.S.? Would a citizen have received a different settlement? Having worked in Peru, she is eligible for a pension. Should she leave the U.S. and retire to Peru?

6. Jose Luis completed three years of college in Mexico. Why do you think he has had difficulty finding employment in the U.S.?

7. We grant political refugees asylum in the U.S. In Laura's Story, do you think having an abusive husband is reason to grant her asylum? Both of Laura's children are in Guatemala. Should she return to be with her children or try to stay in the U.S. and earn money for the future?

8. Although Rocío's parents only completed a few years of school, Rocío graduated from a prestigious American university. How do you think Carmen and his wife helped Rocío achieve her accomplishments? What is Carmen's perception of his daughter and how does it differ from her perception of herself? Do you agree with Rocío's philosophy regarding day laborers? What should Rocío do if/when her DACA status is terminated?

9. Has this book changed your outlook on day workers? On illegal immigrants? If so, how? Have these stories impacted your views on the current U.S. immigration policy? Do you think it is different for each case? Why?

10. In the San Francisco Bay Area, the Day Worker Center of Mountain View is supported by the community and the police. Do you think that this is a good policy, even though many of the workers are undocumented?

11. There are approximately 11 million undocumented immigrants in the U.S. today. What do you think America's policy should be concerning them?

12. In many of the stories, the workers dream of returning to their home country. Do you think they will? If no, why not?

CPSIA information can be obtained
at www.ICGtesting.com
Printed in the USA
FSOW04n0327280716
23116FS